Persevere Past *your* Paralysis

Five Principles of Powering Through Problems in Life

Persevere Past your Paralysis

Five Principles of Powering Through Problems in Life

Dr. James M. Perdue
Professor of Perseverance

Persevere
Past *your*
Paralysis
is a trademark owned by the author.
The author's website:
http://JamesPerdueSpeaks.com
and Email: JamesPerdueSpeaks@comcast.net

The author of this book is not a doctor of medicine and does not dispense medical advice or prescribe the use of any technique as a form of treatment for physical, emotional, or medical problems. The intent of the author is only to offer information of a general nature to help you in overcoming adversities by telling his story along with providing other people's stories. In the event you use any of the information in this book for yourself, the author and the publisher assume no responsibility for your action.

ISBN – 13: 978-0692339985
ISBN – 10: 0692339981

Dedicated to my mom Kate and brother Tim.
Both have overcome adversities in life,
while setting an example to me to
Persevere Past *my* Paralysis.

Dr. Perdue gives you a map that will lead you through most of life's problems. He calls on great leaders and ordinary people as experienced guides as well as his own tested techniques. Follow him to your own personal success.

Shirly Phipps
Retired Educator

The principles from <u>Persevere Past *your* Paralysis</u> are easy to follow because of the simple guidelines. The stories of different types of challenges used in this book proves overcoming adversities can be done. These guidelines will be beneficial during my next challenge in life.

Dennis Parks
Retired Minister

This is the first motivational book I've ever read. Reading it made me realize I could have done a lot better with my life. This would be a great book for parents to start teaching young children about disappointment and grief. It would have been a great book for me to read when my kids were little and had the ability to understand it.

Sue VanBuskirk

I loved Dr. Perdue's latest book! I couldn't put it down. To think of all the heartache and grief some families have to deal with and still they persevere. God works in funny ways; I think He gave Dr. Perdue the ability to write his books to serve as a "wake up call" for a lot of people who think they can't cope with life's unexpected situations. Please keep these great books coming.

Donna Bellis

James Perdue has persevered past his paralysis and so much more. His compassion to help others is evident in his writing. Reading his book is like talking with a friend.

Brenda Moody
LePrint Express

TABLE OF CONTENTS

"We are each on our own journey. Each of us is on our very own adventure; encountering all kinds of challenges, and the choices we make on that adventure will shape us as we go; these choices will stretch us, test us and push us to our limit; and our adventure will make us stronger then we ever know we could be."
Penelope Garcia, Criminal Minds

Chapter 1
Paramount Motivation

Patience and perseverance have a magical effect before which difficulties disappear and obstacles vanish. A little knowledge that acts is worth infinitely more than much knowledge that is idle.
- John Quincy Adams

My childhood dream was to play professional baseball, and working hard on the diamond with the God-given talent for the opportunity was my mission. I earned a baseball scholarship and attended college for only two weeks. On September 11, 1983, a group of us decided to play football on the campus front yard. After about two hours of playing, I decided to quit to get prepared for class the next day.

About ten feet away from the huddle, I heard, "We need someone to run the ball."

After stopping, I turned to my teammates

and said, "I'll come back for one more play."

That play changed my life forever. The ball was handed off to me and with all my strength I burst through the defensive line scoring a touchdown. While putting the ball down and turning left, I saw something coming from my right side. After the play was over, unprepared to be tackled, I heard a loud POP! We both went to the ground and only one of us was able to return to our feet.

With all my power I tried getting up off the ground, but all that would move was my head. Nothing followed – not my shoulders, not my arms, and especially not my legs or feet. Instantly, I was a quadriplegic at the age of nineteen. Three vertebrae in my neck were broken and I sustained a spinal cord injury. There was no movement from my neck down.

Later that night, after being told I would never walk again and possibly might not move from my neck down, my family was informed that providing care for me would be a huge responsibility for them. They might want to think about placing me in a nursing home.

Uncertainty about my future and fear became a recurring feeling about my life. Not knowing if any movement in my limbs would be regained and concerned that movement would not return clouded my every thought. Would I have enough strength to lead an independent life? Mother Teresa said, "Life is a game – play it... Life is too precious, do not destroy it..." Also, legendary basketball coach John Wooden said, "It's not so important who starts the game, but who finishes it." Being the competitor from playing sports, it was time for me to say, "Let the games begin." Napoleon Hill stated with confidence to encourage people, "Every adversity, every failure, every heartache carries with it the seed on an equal or greater benefit."

If I were to ask you, what motivates you? What makes you get up in the mornings? What makes you want to achieve success in life? Could it be your family, children, money, or the desire to want to please others? Could it be your grandfather who was a war hero, or your grandmother who held the family together during the war while your grandfather was gone? Motivation comes in many forms. Real life stories found in books, movies, and music give motivation, along with ideas, to people that could help during difficult times. People are motivated by sports, providing for their family, staying sober, developing the best character as possible. They are self-motivated to not only survive life but also to assist others to overcome adversities.

There are numerous books that you can read for motivation. For example: 1946 book entitled *Man's Search for Meaning, by* Viktor Frankl. The book chronicles his experiences in a Nazi concentration camp and describes his reasons or purpose for living. Even though he lost his wife during that time, he determined his purpose for living was to continue his research when he was freed. Also, he concluded that one of the things this horrendous tragedy could not take away from him was his attitude of how to respond during the dreadful experience. Dave Dravecky's book *The Worth of a Man* is about finding the difference between the bitterness of an unexpected illness and the satisfaction of a man that can still maintain his manly duties such as providing as a husband, father, and friend. Cancer took his left arm, his pitching arm, his moneymaker and family provider, in 1991, which took away his baseball career. Dave was on a journey, searching for his meaning of life. Dennis Byrd played football for the New York Jets and sustained a spinal cord injury in 1992. His book *Rise and Walk: The Trial and*

Triumph of Dennis Byrd relates his relationship with God and his perseverance to walk again.

The movie *Blind Side* provides motivation for people to do the right thing or to provide morals in life by helping the under-privileged. An affluent white family takes in a homeless African American young man who eventually goes to college and becomes a starter in the National Football League. *Brian's Song* is a movie about a professional football player who has cancer and his drive to live so he can come back to the league. He and his best friend Gale Sayers, an African American, both defy the times of segregation in the 1960's to help each other overcome adversities. The movie *127 Hours* is about a hiker who gets trapped between a rock and the wall of a canyon. He trades his arm for his life. His need to live is stronger than the destiny of death.

Music has long been a motivational tool dating back to hymns and carrying into today's types of songs. My brother died at an early-unexpected age. When I hear Garth Brooks' *The Dance* and Vince Gill's *Go Rest High,* they make me remember him. The song by Queen *We Are The Champions* will get any sporting team fired up and motivated to win a championship. I enjoy rooting for the underdog unless they're playing my team.

Sporting events may also motivate people. The shot heard around the world came when the 1951 Giants Bobby Thomson hit the homerun that beat the Brooklyn Dodgers. The 1980 America Olympic hockey team, as featured in *Miracle,* beat the dominating Russian team. The most recent upset came when the New York Giants beat the New England Patriots in Super Bowl LIV. The Patriots were trying to achieve the first undefeated season since the 1972 Miami Dolphins.

People are motivated by self-worth, money; they want to be able to live better than their parents. They are motivated by providing and developing their children's character. They want their children to want for nothing. People grew up watching their own father or mother and grandparents working hard to provide for their families and then end up dying an early life due to working too hard trying to keep up with the Jones'.

Animals provide motivation for people. The need for animals in people's lives is strong. Some pets become a member of the family, while others treat their pets better than their own children. Some pets are treated better than their owners. The pet owner will feed their pets better quality food than they eat themselves. There are many organizations that are motivated to stop and prevent animal cruelty. Animals that have been abused possess their own motivation. Animals show that the will to live is stronger than feeling sorry for themselves or wanting to die. They demonstrate to us that life is too short to feel miserable for ourselves, but living life to the fullest is more desirable. For example, when driving around a curve going to work one morning, and just minutes before I got there a black dog was hit by a car. The dog was paralyzed in the hind legs but the dog was dragging himself by his front legs to get off the road so as not to get hit again. His will to live was stronger than remaining there to die. The love of a pet is unconditional and that might be the only love a person ever received while growing up.

Ricardo, my service canine companion, was a puppy raised in one of Mississippi's prison systems. The inmate who trained him was locked up for whatever reason. He made the comment, "Even though it hurts to give up any dog I helped trained, knowing my educated canine will be assisting someone in need helps me during my troubled times." Some convicts have told others that the dog they trained provided them the unconditional love they never received from their parents. Rarely were they truly happy growing up.

Helen Keller tells us, "Many persons have the wrong idea of what constitutes true happiness. It is not attained through self-gratification, but through fidelity to a worthy purpose." Some people are not happy unless they make others around them miserable. They are so insecure with their lives that they believe a happy life is impossible to attain and they try their best to keep everybody around them in a negative state of mind. They are so caught up in material things, keeping up with the Jones', and/or comparing themselves with other people's materials that they don't realize the greatness they truly live. We can only control our reactions to events in our lives and that is hard enough. So do not place any unneeded pressure on yourself or your family trying to compete with or compare to other people. Be faithful and committed to your family and they will learn to do the same to their families in the future.

Faulkner once said, "Don't bother just to be better than your contemporaries or predecessors. Try to be better than yourself." Look within yourself and see how you have changed for the better over your life. When going through adversities, people will find out how they are truly made. Adversity will make or break people for the good or the bad. As we grow and mature, we change from our experiences during life, the people we associate with, and the environment in which we live. "We are not the same persons this year as last; nor are those we love. It is a happy chance if we, changing, continue to love a changed person," W. Somerset Maugham tells us.

If we look at something other than material objects as a measuring tool in life, then our eyes might be opened to our happiness. Poet Haniel Long said, "So much of what is best in us is bound up in our love of family that it remains the measure of our stability because it measures our sense of loyalty." The love of a family is a great contributor to being able to accept difficulties and defeat problems in life. When children grow up, it is a reflection on the parent's character, guidance, and overall development of them. When growing up, children are taught by their parents on how to deal with challenges. If the child witnesses defeat and giving up, he will more than likely develop a negative behavior but the opposite is true as well. When someone learns how to endure and survive an unfavorable situation early in life, he or she will be prepared to triumph over tragedies in the future.

The behavior of a person, good or bad, is not necessarily the outcome from the parents. It is also the environment in which they were reared, the people who they are trying to influence or have been influencing them, the nutrients or lack of, their genetic makeup and/or other outside contributors. "Behavior is the mirror in which everyone shows their true image," Johann Wolfgang Von Goethe concluded.

What do you consider as your motivation or inspiration, especially after overcoming difficulties? Do you continue to provide for the family? Seek financial independence? Find happiness? Encourage and assist other people who are experiencing or have experienced adversities? Acquire material items? Raise your children? Or you can fill in the blank. "If passion drives you, let reason hold the reins," according to Benjamin Franklin. I believe any answers you respond with or a combination of answers are correct. Not one thing will make you prosperous over problems all the time. What made you successful to overcome difficulties today may not be on your list next year. What made you victorious while in the face of adversities when you were a teenager might not be the same thing when you're fifty or even older.

When talking about overcoming adversities, destroying difficulties, trials and tribulations, disasters, challenges, tests, or any other terms relating to these, I am not referring to any particular type of situation. People go through divorces, financial glitches, automobile accidents, loss of loved ones, health-related issues, and other tragedies in life everyday. There are many and plenty of different circumstances that place us at a disadvantage that we do not consider pleasant. No matter the event, whether a major disaster or a minor inconvenience, we all react to our problems differently. This book is to address all complications no matter how major or minor and/or long-term or short-term misfortunes, and to present strategies to *Persevere Past your Paralysis*. It is not my place to decide who is worse off than anyone else.

The term *Paralysis* does not necessarily mean being paralyzed. It refers to what is keeping you from attaining a desired lifestyle, being successful, or preventing overcoming adversities. What is holding you back? What do you want to achieve? Let us open our minds, open our eyes and open our hearts to have the strength and courage to pursue what we deserve in life.

We all have different imaginations of what success looks and feels like when we succeed over trials and tribulations. "The best and most beautiful things in life cannot be seen or even touched. They must be felt with the heart." Helen Keller stated beautifully. The loss of a child is devastating no matter the age of victim. Joanne's story reveals what motivates or inspires the memories of her son Jacob whose precious life ended way too soon.

Joanne remembers being in church while pregnant with Jacob. A friend told Joanne that her baby would be a peacemaker and he did indeed become that. He was much like his older brother in that he was very outgoing and likeable. Jacob was also like his middle brother in that he was a quick learner. There were never many fights between the brothers, and when they started karate, they became the three musketeers.

Jacob was always a happy boy. When he took his life on October 4, 2007, it caught everybody by surprise. As a fifteen year old, he was going through some frustrating times, but nothing that seemed insurmountable for Jacob. He was having headaches that our family doctor was in the process of evaluating. His girlfriend had recently dumped him, which hurt him deeply. Sadly it was too much for Jacob to bear and he committed suicide. It took several years for Joanne to get over the pain and even now there are times when it hits her like a ton of bricks.

One thing that has helped Joanne deal with this is the story of the Carrot, Egg and Coffee Bean: Which are you? (author unknown) This is how that story goes:

A daughter complained to her father about her life and how things were so hard for her. She did not know how she was going to make it and wanted to give up. She was tired of fighting and struggling. It seemed as soon as one problem was solved, a new one arose.

Her father, a chef, took her to the kitchen.

He filled three pots with water and placed each on a gas burner. Soon the pots came to a boil. In one he placed carrots, in the second he placed eggs, and in the last he placed ground coffee beans. He let them sit and boil, without saying a word. The daughter impatiently waited, wondering what he was doing. In about twenty minutes he got up and turned off the burners. He fished the carrots out and placed them in a bowl. He took the eggs out and placed them a bowl. Then he ladled the coffee out and placed it in a bowl. Turning to her he asked. "Darling, what do you see?"

"Carrots, eggs, and coffee," she replied.

He brought her closer and asked her to feel the carrots. She did and noted that they were soft. He then asked her to take an egg and break it. After pulling off the shell, she observed the hard-boiled egg.

Finally, he asked her to sip the coffee. She smiled, as she tasted its rich aroma. She asked. "What does it mean, Father?"

He explained that each of them had faced the same adversity, boiling water, but each reacted differently. The carrot went in strong, hard, and unrelenting. But after being subjected to the boiling water, it softened and became weak.

The egg had been fragile. Its thin outer shell had protected its liquid interior. But after sitting through the boiling water, its inside became hardened. The ground coffee beans were unique however. After they were in the boiling water, they had changed the water.

"Which are you?" he asked his daughter. "When adversity knocks on your door, how do you respond? Are you a carrot, an egg, or a coffee bean?" How about you?

Are you the carrot that seems hard, but with pain and adversity do you wilt and become soft and lose your strength? Are you the egg, which starts off with a malleable heart? Were you a fluid spirit, but after a death, a breakup, or a layoff have you become hardened and stiff? Your shell looks the same, but are you bitter and tough with a stiff spirit and heart? Or are you like the coffee bean? The bean changes the hot water, the thing that is bringing the pain. When the water gets the hottest, it just tastes better. If you are like the bean, when things are at their worst, you get better and make things better around you.

Jacob loved coffee and his favorite place to hang was Starbucks. So what helps Joanne the most is focusing on being the bean. When memories overwhelm her, she becomes the bean.

Joseph Campbell made a comment, "Find a place inside where there's joy, and the joy will burn out the pain." By being the bean, it gives Joanne the strength to go on, the much needed strength to continue to take care of her family, even when it seems too hard. Even when the emotions of the loss are strong, she must be the bean. Focusing on being the bean is an inner thing that just flows out.

Joanne took an unimaginable situation and uses a special but simple technique to recall the memories of her son Jacob. The aroma of a peppermint cup of coffee allows her, even just for a minute, to escape the day-to-day hassle of life and reminisce about the good old days with Jacob. Many people have expressed that the smell or taste of something brings back memories. Something as simple as the smell of peppermint or the taste of chocolate can bring huge rewards such as great memories.

Suicide is a serious problem with our youth. People need to recognize the symptoms and refer the individual for immediate help.

The main ingredient to motivation lies

within us. We have to be self-motivated to succeed and overcome challenges in life. "When you want to succeed as bad as you want to breathe, then you'll be successful," Eric Thomas, former football player, stated. When we decide on what we want to accomplish, we must maintain focus and we must have clear objectives. Staying focused and fired-up may be easier said than done. With everything happening in our lives we can be easily distracted and we can lose concentration on the main goal. By having precise clear goals, we will find it easier to stay focused and motivated to get the best out of ourselves.

Abraham Lincoln said, "Whatever you are, be a good one." I'm going to give you my secrets to overcoming adversities. Believe it or not, we are not designed to suffer for nothing. There are lessons to learn in life: we find out how strong we are emotionally, mentally, physically, and spiritually, how bad we desire something, the need for challenges, and the aspiration to help others less fortunate. We need to be reminded of what we already know it takes to overcome difficulties and be successful. My five P's are what aided me to achieve and appreciate a rich life.

The reasons for my success to triumph over tragedies have been instilled in me since I was a child. While believing in God, then I was born with the desire to have abundance and there is a plan for my future. My family members modeled to me the attitude to be a winner, the determination to deal with difficulties, the needed preparation that is required to be successful, and the understanding to accept change.

My five P's for success in life and overcoming adversities are: having a purpose in life, taking personal responsibility, having partner(s) for support, finding the power needed from within yourself, and persevering. In this book there will be stories of struggles used as examples to demonstrate it can be done. There will be inspirational quotes from people who have been successful and lead a good life, despite their differences. I've used these five P's for success to remind myself of the hard work, fortitude, and the fight that is needed to get past adversities.

Body builder champion Arnold Schwarzenegger stated with confidence, "For me life is continuously being hungry. The meaning of life is not simply to exist, to survive, but to move ahead, to go up, to achieve, to conquer."

I hope this book will encourage you to get fired up to have a successful and enjoyable life as you Persevere Past *your* Paralysis.

Strategies to Implement:

1. Sign up on a website. You might want two or three different sites that will e-mail positive quotes or Bible scriptures, and inspiring short stories. On YouTube, subscribe to motivational videos.
2. Read motivational or inspirational articles, books, or magazines at least once a month. If you are not a reader, there are plenty of books on audio.
3. Do you need to do all of these positive building strategies? No. With time being a virtue, you might want to do one strategy a day. Rotate each one so it will not be boring or repetitive.
4. During the day, focus on the positive so to train your mind to remain optimistic.

Finally, brothers and sisters, rejoice! Strive for

*full restoration, encourage one another, be of
one mind, live in peace.
And the God of love and peace will be with you.
2 Corinthians 13:11*

Chapter 2
Purpose of Your Life

Learn to get in touch with the silence within yourself, and know that everything in life has purpose. There are no mistakes, no coincidences, all events are blessings given to us to learn from.
- Elisabeth Kubler-Ross

What is your purpose? Sometimes this question is easier to ask than it is to answer. Finding your purpose might take a lifetime, but once it is found, put forth all your effort. As we grow and learn about ourselves, we might begin to understand our purpose. Make a list of things you enjoy doing. You might want to ask a few friends to help with the list. They might think of something you're good at that you didn't remember. Then cross out any thing that you really enjoy doing but feels like work. Study what's left on the list and see if there is anything on it that could be your purpose.

Sometimes our purpose is placed on us through tragedies such as being hit by a drunk driver. So your mission in life is to educate people about the effects of driving drunk. Maybe a family member is fighting cancer so you want to be the one to find a cure. The death of a child would be detrimental to anyone but it could lead someone toward his or her purpose in life.

Not having any children of my own, the death of a child is unimaginable but the stress of the loss is understandable. My younger brother passed way two weeks before his thirty-eighth birthday. Watching my mother contain her emotions and thoughts from the stress was impressive. Whether the child is young or older, the parents feel sorry but also guilty because they feel the child is supposed to bury them not the other way around. In the long run of life, this type of tragedy is never forgotten but sometimes a positive outcome occurs.

When a major ordeal takes place in our lives, it usually leaves an impression. It could be a physical reminder of a particular incident such as being burnt, suffering an amputation, or becoming paralyzed. Maybe stress from a terrible situation could enhance mental or emotional problems: such as an automobile accident, overindulgent of drugs or alcohol, or loss of a loved one, especially if it is a child. These types of marks are continuous remembrances of what took place in our past, but by having a positive attitude, people can still live a good life. Rose Kennedy said with compassion, "It has been said, 'time heals all wounds.' I do not agree. The wounds remain. In time, the mind, protecting its sanity, covers them with scar tissue and the pain lessens. But it is never gone." Unfortunate events could lead you to your purpose.

As hard as it might be to conceive, try to view the physical impairment as a blessing; think positive. Yes, it will be hard and may take a long time. After losing the use of my legs and knowing the life I had known at that time was dead but not gone forever, I had to recover. I have been fortunate to live my lifestyle. Before my injury, earning a college degree was not in my interest, whereas traveling to Africa to be an ambassador for people with disabilities was never a thought either but, as it turns out, educating people about disabilities awareness is one of my purposes.

Even though having a physical

impairment may be difficult to comprehend, a mental or emotional condition could be worse. If the mental or emotional disorder cannot be controlled, there are institutions, counseling, medicine, and combinations of the three that can assist in living as normal a life as possible. No matter how small the emotional or mental damage may seem, there can be an enormous consequences such as, the lack of understanding from a particular episode in life. If you were Ron, how would you deal with life in this next story?

Ron started life in a much different way than most babies. He was born with a bad heart. The first few weeks of his life were touch and go. When the doctors declared him strong enough to withstand surgery, a life saving procedure was performed. During open-heart surgery, Ron's natural valves were replaced with pigs' valves.

The first few years of Ron's life his parents pretty much placed him in a bubble. They were very protected of him and were scared every time Ron explored his surrounding as a child. As he got older, Ron's parents lifted the protection shield so Ron could live as normal as possible.

He played in the dirt, mud and anywhere a growing boy wanted to investigate his interest. In elementary school Ron wasn't feeling good and his doctor determined he needed another heart surgery. This was Ron's second heart procedure in his short life and sadly it won't be his last.

Ron recovered from surgery as predicted and his parents decided not to baby him. He was going to live his life as normal as possible. Ron's father liked baseball so he started throwing a ball with Ron in hopes he would like to play someday.

As he grew, Ron was able to perform with his schoolmates. He made good grades, made friends, went out with different girls and became a standout baseball player. In Little League baseball, Ron pitched for his team, was one of the better hitters in the league, and made the all-star team. He enjoyed baseball as much as his dad liked watching him play.

After graduating from high school, Ron tried college but felt it wasn't for him. One good thing did happen while attending higher education, Ron found his future wife. When they met he explained about his heart issues and she explained about her muscular disease, Multiple

Sclerosis. Even though both of them had major health problems, not only did they marry but they also had a healthy child despite the odds.

Ron tried to provide for his family by working as a store clerk and later became a security guard while his wife stayed home raising their boy. Their marriage lasted about three years, and like some others, they divorced. As life continued, Ron was trying to find his purpose in life.

After struggling to maintain employment, Ron felt as if his life was drowning in disappointment and uncertainty. As hard as he tried to break away from life's challenging bear hug, it seemed he couldn't do anything right. He became depressed and started drinking to help him forget about his problems.

Even though his drinking continued, Ron married again and had another healthy son. As Ron was getting on his feet in life, disaster happened again. At the age of twenty-seven, he had his third open-heart surgery. Because of the abuse Ron placed on his body by drinking, smoking and being overweight, it was harder for his body to overcome the operation.

After months of being in the hospital, Ron went home to continue recovery. During that time he made a complete transformation, mentally and physically. Ron quit smoking, stopped drinking and lost weight. His attitude was completely overhauled as well. He was positive about his outcome and soon found his purpose in life.

He studied and passed all requirements to be a truck driver. He could be the best father to both of his children, while providing assistance to his ex-wife so her life would be easier, because her health was declining and she was placed in a nursing home. Ron's second wife even joined him in helping with his ex-wife. Buddha was once quoted, "A family is a place where minds come in contact with one another. If these minds love one another, the home will be as beautiful as a flower garden. But if these minds get out of harmony with one other it is like a storm that plays havoc with the garden."

The next three years Ron felt like a prize-winning pig. His second life opportunity as a family provider, along with raising his first-born, was as rare as teeth on a chicken's beak. For the first time in Ron's life, he was excited about his future.

At the age of thirty, Ron's heart failed him for the last time, but not before he found his purpose in life. "Everything in the universe has a purpose. Indeed, the invisible intelligence that flows through everything in a purposeful fashion is also flowing through you," according to Wayne Dyer.

Ron had finally discovered happiness in his world by being unselfish and supporting others rather than pleasing himself. He left this world a better place for his offspring while knowing they could be a blessing to others.

It's hard to come back from struggles in life but to start your life with a major problem is even more difficult. To overcome any adversity is an awesome experience, but to discover your purpose, even though you have a lifelong health issue, is a miracle. The odds were greatly against Ron from the beginning but after learning his life's mission he was able to roll with the punches.

Like Ron, we must discover our life purpose. Even though his life started off rocky, it is never too late to find the ultimate purpose in life. Stephen Hawking, wheelchair bound because of Amyotrophic lateral sclerosis (ALS), better known as Lou Gehrig's Disease, brilliantly said, "However difficult life may seem, there is always something you can do and succeed at."

Is there more than one purpose in life? Yes, I believe as we grow and learn from life, our long-term purposes or life's missions change. We should have short-term purposes as well. We all wear different hats in life such as being a father or mother, a single parent, a widow, a son or daughter, a provider, a nephew or niece, a friend, college student and in my case a person living with a disability. You should have goals that align with each label you carry. Don't just think about the goals, WRITE them down so you can reflect on them as needed. For some of the goals you want to achieve, you should write the date you produced them and fill in the date when the objective has been accomplished. There should be short-term goals that align with the long-term goal or goals. These short-term goals will help you stay focused on the ultimate purpose and when they are achieved it feels like a win or victory. These wins keep you fired up. For example:

> Long-term goal: September 11, 1983, was the date I became paralyzed, so by September 11, 1988, I want to be as independent as possible for as long as possible in

my life. *Completed 1986. Two years ahead of schedule.*

Short-term goals: At the end of 1984, feeding myself consistently till feeding myself all the time. *Feeding myself before the end of 1984.*

Dressing myself with little to no assistance from other people by the middle of 1985. Took longer. *Dressing myself in 1986.*

Transferring in and out of bed by myself by the end of 1985. *On schedule according to target date.*

Taking full care of my personal hygiene which includes brushing my teeth, getting in and out of the shower by myself, and emptying my bowel and bladder by the end of 1985. *A lot of work, but accomplished all by the end of 1985.*

Return to driving a vehicle as soon as possible. *It took two years but I gained a big part of independence by driving again.*

Graduating from a college or university is a huge challenge that few ever succeed. Another example of writing goals and placing dates after completing them can look like this as a college student is progressing through his or her course work. Use the college's catalog because the course's requirements to graduate are already set up. Write the long-term and short-term goals in the margin or upper and lower sections of the book. When completing a class write the semester and year along with the final grade.

Long-term goal is to graduate.

Short-term goals are to sign up for classes and complete assignments with the best grade possible.

English 101 *Fall*   *2010 A*
English 201
Math 101   *Spring*   *2009 B*
Math 201

Literature 101
Literature 201   *Summer*   *2010* A

As you can see, the dates are aligned with the earned grade for each course. This is good for two reasons. One reason is there is a clear view on classes taken and passed. Instead of crossing out the course with a marker and making your catalog messy, this way it is easy to determine the next classes needed when it is time to register. The other reason is, by viewing the grades, it gives you confidence and encouragement knowing how far you have come from the beginning and knowing the light at the end is not a moving train to derail you. Always placing the semester, date and grade allows you to know how close graduation ceremony is approaching.

Remember, we have different hats all throughout life so a one-size fit all may not work. Be open and honest on what your desires are while being prepared to work hard on achieving those goals. Include others to help arrange or develop your goals and do not get overwhelmed if you fall short on a goal.

Everything is going great and your goals are being met with encouragement because of the assistance from family and friends. What do you do if there is a date set for a goal and it has not been achieved? For example from the above list – Dressing myself with little to no assistance from other people by the middle of 1985. It took longer than expected. Achieved dressing myself in 1986.

Do you give up on that goal and dump it? Do you learn from what you have accomplished and continue shooting for the victory? The choice is up to you. It may depend on how that goal will aid you in the long-term. If the goal is dropped, can the long-term or other purposes still be completed? If yes, then you might want to delete it. If no, you will need to adjust the goal and/or extend the completion date. Dressing myself was so important to me that even though it took longer than desired it was worth it.

For any purpose or life's mission involving the family or other people, it is better to have everybody put their two cents in to prepare the goals. With everyone involved, there is a better chance of the objects to be followed. Since it is a long-term goal, as everybody involved grows older and more mature there will be a need to adjust the statement as each purpose has been accomplished. Look at the statement once a year with everyone who helped develop it. Talk about what was attained last year, what needs to be added for the future and what needs to be rewritten for clarity to make the goal manageable for the people involved.

Part of my long-term goal is to help, encourage, and/or assist my fellow man or woman whenever possible. According to Lewis Carroll, "One of the deep secrets of life is all that is really worth doing is what we do for others." Also, Albert Pine said, "What we do for ourselves dies with us. What we do for others and the world remains and is immortal."

Notice the final part of the long-term goal statement, *whenever possible*, because as much as we would like, we by ourselves, cannot help every group, organization, cause, or person in need. We can only do so much by giving financial assistance or volunteering. If we try to give or help every cause, then we will neglect our needs and responsibilities. By not being able to take care of our needs, we surely will not be able to contribute to the ones we feel strongly about.

We can pick and choose the associations and institutions that best support our beliefs. Since sustaining a spinal cord injury, one foundation I support is a cure for neurology disorders and other related research. Also, I support Canine Companion for Independence because of the trained canine they provided to me.

As we grow-up, throughout our lives we will experience multiple short-term purposes. Goals can help us be sure we are on the right track to being the best we can be. Early in life, I wanted to be a trash collector, cowboy, fireman, and finally a professional baseball player.

To become a professional ball player, part of my goal was to practice, practice, practice. Along with becoming a professional, special skills are required with the desire to work hard. Less than one percent of athletes ever make it to the big dance. It finally comes down to the best player and the ones who were close enough but not quite good enough watch it on television.

Other short-term purposes might be marriage and family life (hopefully these is a long-term purpose but with our society and the divorce rate it does not look good), careers, staying sober from alcohol and/or drugs, different friends through life, survivor of a disease, become a widow, going from rich and losing everything or the opposite going from rags to riches are a few examples. If goals are developed, with everyone involved having an input, the better the goals will provide guidance and a better chance of succeeding.

Sometimes we have a choice in the short-term purpose while other times it is decided for us. With every inch of my power, becoming a professional baseball player was my desire, aspiration, ambition, and goal. But sometimes life kicks you right in the mouth and your purpose in life changes – fast.

"Who knows where inspiration comes from. Perhaps it arises from desperation. Perhaps it comes from the flukes of the universe, the kindness of the muses" wisely stated Amy Tan. After an unexpected hit during a football game, playing baseball was no longer a choice in life. Instantly being paralyzed from the neck down changed my purpose of playing baseball to surviving and living the cards that were dealt to me. Sometimes our purpose is handed to us.

Living in this world is hard enough when life goes unchallenged. As long as our journey is a smooth ride we can enjoy what life has to offer. That would be great, but we know life is tough and the old adage, "Life is not fair" we learn at an early age.

Some of us are our own worst enemy because we listen too much to what other people are saying and doing. We focus on what we have no control over in life and we worry over the little things; you know we sweat the small stuff. Sigmund Wollman tells us, "If you break your neck, if you have nothing to eat, if your house is on fire—then you got a problem. Everything else is inconvenience. Life *is* inconvenient. Life *is* lumpy. Learn to separate the inconveniences from the real problems. You will live longer."

People have talked themselves out of living their dreams due to self-destruction. The little things get in their way. According to Anatole France, "To accomplish great things, we must not only act, but also dream; not only plan, but also believe."

We should plan and hope for the best for the future while preparing for the worst. Steve Nash, a professional basketball player, once said, "You have to rely on your preparation. You got to really be passionate and try to prepare more than anyone else, and put yourself in a position to succeed, and when the moment comes you got to enjoy, relax, breathe and rely on your preparation so that you can perform and not be anxious or filled with doubt." When complications are on the way we can be prepared. We cannot be ready for everything, but when we survive a challenge we are better prepared for the next difficulty. Thich Nhat Hanh suggests, "Hope is important because it can make the present moment less difficult to bear. If we believe that tomorrow will be better, we can bear a hardship today."

When the next nuisance happens try not to freak out, but sit back, relax and prioritize the situation. Only you know if the circumstance is a minor or major emergency. In the middle of the night, you get thirsty so when getting out of bed and walking to the kitchen to get water in the dark your stump you toe against the door way. Is this a minor or major crisis? Only you know. If you are healthy, then the painful toe is probably a minor situation. On the other hand, if you have brittle bone disease, or you have hemophilia, or you have Progeria, a rare disease where your body ages too fast, then stumping your toe could be a major emergency. Again, only you know what constitutes a minor or major challenge in life.

Of course, there are no simple answers to an emergency, you inherit a disease, you are addicted to drugs or alcohol, an unexpected financial change by losing your employment, a divorce, and plenty of other events happen in life. When a major disaster happens get a great support system in place. You will need your spouse, best friends, doctors, including a psychologist or psychiatrist. Find someone who has gone through the circumstance so you will have an idea how to prepare, get the church involved with prayer and any other support group who specializes in your world-changing threat. When you are slapped upside your head with an unexpected challenge take steps so you can try and control the situation. "You do not develop courage by being happy in your relationships everyday. You develop it by surviving difficult times and challenging adversity" stated by Epicurus.

If you determine the hazard is minor, such as getting a flat tire but fortunately there were no accidents, do not freak out! It is out of your control. Yes, you will probably be late for your appointment. Change the tire or call someone for help and look at the bright side of this minor problem. Maybe this is a teachable lesson on patience. You know; slow down and smell the roses. Educate your children that life can throw a curve ball but with a positive attitude they can make the best of it.

Most of us find our purpose in life early. For others, they may take longer to figure out the ultimate scheme. They may wander around misguided with no understanding of why certain things happen to them. Bobby's story is one type of survival that most could not and would not want to endure.

Bobby only has a seventh grade education and an alcohol addiction. He is one of those people who easily lose his temper after an excessive consumption of beer. When hitting his limit of alcohol Bobby would do stupid stuff that eventually put him in jail or prison. After three Driving Under the Influences, several assault charges, and not complying with probation, before Bobby knew it, at the age of forty-three he had spent over half his life locked up.

Thirty days in the county jail, up to five years in state penitentiary, on and off probation with a brief six months to two years out of trouble in between incarcerations was Bobby's routine. During each pre-lock up, he would drink and get angry until the inevitable happened; back to cross bars hotel.

Can you image being imprisoned by a drink that most people can consume and make responsible decisions? Not a one-time mistake or even two-time error but half your life miscalculations that Bobby could never relive for the better. Fyodor Dostoyevsky said, "The mystery of human existence lies not in just staying alive, but in finding something to live for."

While in prison, Bobby was able to take a course as a mechanic. He was good using his hands and liked problem-solving. At the age of forty-six, Bobby had been able to stay out of trouble with the help of sobriety. It only took being locked up for over twenty years for him to figure that excessive alcohol plus uncontrollable rage equals time in the pokey. He has been alcohol free for years and has started his own business as a mechanic along with having side jobs mowing lawns. Tony Robbins concluded, "One reason so few of us achieve what we truly want is that we never direct our focus; we never concentrate our power. Most people dabble their way through life, never deciding to master anything in particular."

Even though what seems an eternity, Bobby was able to find his purpose in life as he helps people in need. "It takes half your life before you discover life is a do-it-yourself project," as Napoleon Hill once said. Sadly it took a long time for Bobby but as it is said, "better late than never."

So why not discover and develop a purpose in life? Define your purpose in life. What do you want to do more than anything else? What is your passion? What is the desire in your heart? Once you have figured out your life purpose, then you need to determine if this is really what you want to do. Galileo reveals, "All truths are easy to understand once they are discovered. The point is to discover them." As you discover your purpose it will be the beginning to Persevere Past *your* Paralysis.

Strategies to Implement:

1. Take a piece of paper or use your computer and develop your long-term goal or mission statement. Be sure everyone is involved with the decisions and development of the objects.
2. Design your short-term goals. Place the date with the goals after you are satisfied with the conclusions.
3. Periodically, review the goals to be sure you are on the right track. After

an objective has been achieved, put the date beside the goal and celebrate.

4. If you find there is a goal that is not working out like you want, re-evaluate the situation and decide whether it is important enough to continuing chasing.

5. Develop a plan to better assure your goals are being met.

6. When the next challenge happens in life try to prioritize it. Look at the circumstance surrounding it and it might be a blessing in disguise.

7. Learn from the difficulty and use it as a teachable moment. People can learn from how they deal with trials and tribulations.

Efforts and courage are not enough without purpose and direction.
- John F. Kennedy

Dr. James M. Perdue

Chapter 3
Personal Responsibility for Your Life

"Don't let mental blocks control you. Set yourself free. Confront your fear and turn the mental blocks into building blocks."
- Roopleen

Becoming a leader is not easy, but it is necessary. You need to be the leader of your own life before you can lead other people. If you do not have a strong control on your life, there is someone out there who will control you. Jim Rohn said, "If you don't design your own life plan, chances are you'll fall into someone else's plan. And guess what they have planned for you? Not much." There are lots of stories where people with low self-esteem are controlled emotionally, mentally, physically, and/or spiritually by manipulation and/or abuse. Be sure to know the differences between controlling your life and trying to control uncontrollable things in life.

You have the final say or decision on how to react to any circumstance that affects your life, while trying to control life. You cannot stop the rain; you cannot prevent everybody from driving recklessly; and you definitely cannot stop all the drunk drivers, but you can control when an undesirable event happens, how you respond. You can act negatively which could add to the problem or you can be positive. Being positive gives you a chance to calm down and think rationally about what is needed to conquer the circumstance. Tim's story is a good example of taking control over his life to assure good things will come his way. This is a great story not only for African Americans but also for all people who want a better future for themselves and their generations.

My brother Tim, known as "Bear," and I coached a minor league baseball team in 1980. This league was started to develop players who were not drafted to play Little League and/or were just starting to learn the game of baseball. Bear was seventeen years old while I was sixteen and one of our players was Tim, a ten year old African American, not that being an African

American meant anything to Bear or me but knowing this information is vital later. Tim was the catcher and cleanup hitter for our team. We finished the season undefeated winning fifteen games with no losses. We played the other league champs from across town for the City Championship, and we prevailed.

Being a few years older than Tim, he and other players from the league watched me play high school baseball. I had my own little fan club. Tim's mother also drove the bus when the high school team traveled so keeping up with Tim as he grew up was easy. Every time I learned how much he was accomplishing in life it made me proud to have been his first coach.

Tim graduated from high school in 1989 and played on the state runner-up football team. Tim attended West Point where he not only studied but he also played football. Whenever I see Tim's father in town, he always tells other people that because of Bear and me is why Tim is the man he is today. Obviously, after thanking him for the utmost complement, in reality it's the raising from his parents that gave Tim the character, positive mind set and the desire to succeed in life. Tim graciously gives credit by saying, "I'd like to acknowledge that everything that I've accomplished is only by the Grace of a Loving God through His Son Jesus Christ. Without Him none of this would be possible."

Our newspaper picked up Tim's story of graduating from West Point and the story was buried in the back of the first section of the paper. A woman who was in a car accident along with other negative stories was on the front page. What the hell? You can't be serious! Our society is so concerned about what's wrong in the world instead of granting us a positive story in our lives. The media runs stories with gunshots, automobile disasters, stealing, drug busts and people disrespecting each other all the time.

Please don't misunderstand my point, there are times when its essential to report wrong happenings or disasters such as child abductions, murderer on the loose, escaped prisoner, severe weather, but not a vehicle hit and run with no injuries, a missing dog, undercover drug bust or a prostitution sting. We need more positive stories, for example, a community raising money for a child who needs a heart-lung transplant, repairing homes for the elderly, raising awareness and research money for cures for diseases and other inflictions or how a homeless person got back on his or her feet.

Maybe a story of how a young black man overcomes all sorts of stigmas and challenges who can be a role model for not just the African American population but also to all people. According to Joseph Campbell, "We must be willing to get rid of the life we planned so as to have the life that is waiting for us."

After reading Tim's story, and taking an extensive search to find it in the back of the paper, I contacted the editor and expressed my disbelief. Not only was this story full of perseverance, hard work, and overcoming disadvantages but it also was a great motivator for African Americans and any other people who want to succeed. Wake up, newspaper, you missed the boat on this story.

Why would I open with a negative outcome? We are slowly being programed to view negative events as part of our nature. Society has conditioned us to accept undesirable actions as a big part of life. Yes, providing people live long enough, whether a day old or one hundred years old, bad things will happen. Hopefully, when challenges occur we learn from them and they make us a better person. H. G.

Wells goes on to say, "Affliction comes to us, not to make us sad but sober; not to make us sorry but wise."

Have you ever wondered why some people are successful and why others seem to have a hard time in life? Even when challenges and difficulties happen, they seem to handle them with amazing confidence. Not that anyone wishes tragedies on another person, at least not any normal person would, and sometimes life travels with a blow that most observers say that they could not have gotten through the circumstance. What makes some people deal with adversities with a positive attitude while others seem to drown in the water of self-pity?

After years of watching and being around people, I've concluded there are two types of people in this world. One type is the "I'll sit back and wait for the world to give me something" and the next type is the "go-getters" who believe you do not get something for nothing – "there's no such thing as a free lunch," says Milton Friedman.

The first group of people believes the world and other people owe them something. They seem to be dependent on people because of or a combination of an emotional, a financial, a mental, a physical, or a spiritual need. Usually they lack self-confidence and may question all decisions they make. They were born to their situations or they acquired it later in life.

Since becoming disabled, I might seem biased using these examples. Research has shown that people born with a disability enjoy and accept their lifestyle better than those who acquire their disability later in life. When a child is born with a disability the family provides support and positively interacts with the child. Children learn even though they are different from other people and a healthy lifestyle is attainable. When people are disabled later in life, they may view life as being over because they witnessed how other people made fun of people with disabilities. They find it harder to provide for the family, or they cannot enjoy life as one who is disabled because of the attached stigma.

They wait for opportunities to come to them and they can't understand why they struggle in life. Some people believe their destiny is to struggle in all forms of life. They do the same work as their parents because this is all they know, even though their parents told them there is a better life. Sometimes the children feel guilty if they receive a better life than their parents. They have false thoughts that people will condemn them if they do better in life.

Whenever someone has mental problems, the world seems too demanding and they might struggle to stay afloat in life. Other people seem to drive them down even more by telling them they are wasting their time. The naysayer can brainwash people by telling them it's impossible to have a better life.

Sometimes people believe more in their friend's opinion than in their own inner strength, confidence and logic. They think that their friends and family know them best. No. You know yourself better than anyone else. You know what you are capable of doing. Believe in yourself, be confident, make sure your faith is strong and no matter what comes, you will be able to deal with the situation. "For those who believe, no proof is necessary. For those who don't believe, no proof is possible," Stuart Chase was quoted. If you do not believe in yourself, how can you know if you are using the best judgments to make the right decisions for your life? According to Karl Kraus, "A weak man has doubts before a decision. A strong man has them afterwards."

They get comfortable in life. If I try and fail, then my time, money, and energy were wasted. I do not want to start over again. If they fall, they believe they should have listened to the negative people. Besides, their destiny is to work hard and struggle.

The other type of people is the ones that are "go-getters." They get what they believe is theirs in life. They believe in hard work, they sacrifice in life, they take responsibility for their lives, and they help other people by giving them a helping hand not a handout. They believe in their dreams, their purpose in life, and they work hard until they attain their goals in life. Even when their goals are not achieved or fall short of their dreams, they do not give up. They take responsibility for their lives and figure out a way to reach their destination in life.

"I am not concerned that you have fallen. I am concerned that you arise," according to Abraham Lincoln. Sometimes we must fail to be successful; it lets us know if we really want what we desire, we learn from failure. Sometime struggles will come with future benefits. Being successful is not easy; being successful does not come without a price. When we are unsuccessful or challenged in a way we are not prepared for, we learn from it. We find out how strong we are; we can build on the failure to become successful. Failure can trigger a new idea, and we become stronger and more confident when the next adversity comes in our lives.

When deciding something new such as employment, dating, traveling to a different country, or a necessary medical procedure, collect as much information as possible to help with making the best decision possible. Collect as much information from your spouse, family, friends, and the World Wide Web so you can be better prepared. The more you are educated about anything, the more confident you will be to do what's best for you and your life.

Keeping a positive attitude will aid you more in life than being negative. By being negative, you worry too much, your stress level rises, and you are not as happy as you would like to be. According to Zig Ziglar, "Positive thinking will let you do everything better than negative thinking will." A positive thinking person handles challenges with optimism, starts the day with hope, provides assurance to everybody, he approaches life that is worth living, and believes no matter the contests in life he will eventually win.

Break away from the negative people; get out of your comfort zone; take some risks in life. Surround yourself with people who will encourage you to do better, people who will help you attain your goals in life. Be confident in your dreams and push yourself harder until you reach your dream. Pearl Bailey communicated, "You never find yourself until you face the truth."

After being told I would never walk again, possibly not move from my neck down, my family was advised to place me in a nursing home. I started thinking. What will I do with my life? After all, I met JT who was nursing home bound in his late twenties because of an automobile accident. I just knew nursing home here I come. Nursing home was not an option for me and thankfully neither was it for my family. Thankfully, while being reared by my mother, father, brothers and grandparents they instilled in me the need to take responsibility for my life. Fortunately, they did not abandon my needs after the accident to leave me alone for the lifestyle that seemed to be my destiny, but instead they added encouragement, strength, and sacrifice for me to persevere in life.

Tim took personal responsibility for his education and life during his time at West Point, not only graduating but also excelling to the best of his ability. Not that his heritage was bad, but he visioned something more – a better future. Franklin D. Roosevelt communicated to his fellow humans; "Men are not prisoners of fate, but only prisoners of their own minds."

His mother, father, siblings, relatives, friends and coaches influenced him enough so that he knew there was more in life and it is far better than he could imagine. His decisions to take personal responsibility not only to demonstrate to other African American young males they can do better in their lives but also they did not have to live the life with the negative stigma. With an open mind and staying positive, along with assistance from others who believe in you, anything is possible.

Tim's high school guidance counselor had enough faith in his abilities that she first suggested West Point as an option for an education. According to Benjamin Disraeli, "The greatest good you can do for another, is not to share your own riches, but to reveal to him, his own." If you do not hold yourself accountable for your life then who will? Take personal responsibility for your success, happiness, and becoming triumphant over tragedies in your life while you Persevere Past *your* Paralysis.

Strategies to Implement:

1. Make a list of what you have control over in life and compare it to another list of what you have no control over.
2. After comparing the two lists, prioritize what is most important to the least important.
3. Remember, don't sweat the small stuff.

In everything he did he had great success, because the Lord was with him.
1 Samuel 18:14

Dr. James M. Perdue

Chapter 4
Partners in Life

Our prime purpose in this life is to help others. And if you can't help them, at least don't hurt them.
- Dalai Lama

We are placed on this Earth to serve each other whether in need or not. We do not have to face challenges on our own. The people who seem to have it all together have partners or a support group in their lives during tough times. They may be able to afford the best assistance but that doesn't mean others with less funding have to do without.

There is plenty of free and low charging groups or organizations that are specialized in your area of need. After you have benefitted from the counseling or assistance, you might be motivated to work or at least volunteer with the organization so you can help others in their time of desperation.

It might take months or even years for you to gain the reassurance from your partners that its okay to live your life after a significant challenge. "Nothing is permanent in this wicked world— not even our troubles" says Charles Chaplin. By developing your confidence, self-esteem and awareness from your disaster, you can hold your head up high when battling the next catastrophic episode with poise and bravery knowing your partners will be there. Sometimes we have to go through the storm to enjoy the beauty of the coming day. Francis Bacon once commented, "In order for the light to shine so brightly, the darkness must be present."

There might be a partner in your life who will surprise you. Be sure to explore all options when considering someone in your support group and have an open mind. For example, one Saturday morning while transferring out of bed to my wheelchair, it seemed to have had a mind of its own and it rolled out from under me. After falling to the floor like a sack of potatoes, I found out the phone that was three feet away from me was out of reach. What a way to start the weekend; what's the saying? "I've fallen and can't get up." And I didn't have the emergency calling device to request assistance. Not only on the floor without an alert bracelet, but also no one was expecting me on that cool morning.

While lying there, I wondered how long I'd be on the floor before anyone missed me. After cussing and crying, I prepared myself for a big adventure to start the day. I dragged myself from my bedroom to the living room so I could use the phone to call for help. After pulling with my arms, head, chin, and pushing with my legs, it took a burst of energy to maneuver my limited strength body one to three inches at a time. I would then rest five to ten minutes before exerting myself again. The twenty-five foot trip only took two and a half hours. With cuts and scratches on my face, legs, and arms as proof of my battle wounds, I made a victorious call to the EMTs for assistance and as a reward a much-needed rest on the floor was well earned.

On Monday, two people asked what happened to me over the weekend. The first person made a comment that he would have just lay on the floor and waited for someone to come. I explained to him, let's say you lay on the floor for two and a half hours waiting for someone or anyone to visit. During that valuable but wasted time and no visitor entered your home, when do you start the journey?

Now, two and a half hours have gone by with no one knowing you are on the floor so you decide to begin the voyage? After the late start, now you have been on the floor for five hours. Again, I asked, "When do you decide to do something/anything to get help?"

For me, "I start immediately," was my response, with respect.

The second person that asked about my weekend had a better strategy. "James, you need to get one of those dogs that can bring a phone to you. This would solve the problem in case it ever happens again," she said wisely.

Five years earlier, I considered a dog for an assistant. After going over the required paperwork, it was my decision that other people with disabilities were more deserving of receiving a dog on duty due to the lack of their abilities. The paperwork was never submitted.

She replied, "How's that conclusion of not applying for a helping dog working for you now?"

The next day, she gave me information that her niece related to her. It was a website of an organization that trains dogs for people like me who need some assistance to continue living an independent life. Canine Companion for Independence (CCI) trains dogs for people with different disabilities who need different assistants.

After getting on Canine Companion for Independence's website, I started the process of obtaining a trained canine. There were four phases to not only complete but also pass to successfully receive a trained dog. Even though each phase was accomplished, there was a disclaimer stated in all the letters, "Congratulations on passing this phase of the program. Passing each phase and moving on to the next step of the process does not guarantee a canine will be available."

Although completing all phases, it took a year or better for CCI to determine they found the right match for me. After waiting patiently, okay, maybe there was some frustration during the wait; I was introduced to my companion Ricardo. He is my first canine companion and I couldn't have asked for a better partner.

It didn't take long for Ricardo to earn his keep. While transferring into my wheelchair, somehow I was trapped in limbo, half of me was on my wheelchair and the other was half off. With nowhere to go but down on the floor, which I refused to go because of knowing how hard it would be to place me back in the chair. Reaching for my cell phone on my bed didn't pan out as planned. On to the floor the cell phone fell.

It was time to put Ricardo's training into action. "Ricardo, get the phone!" One of Ricardo's forty known commands was given as I pointed under the bed.

He dropped to the floor and dove under the bed like a bird sticking its head in a hole to get a worm. Ricardo backed out from under the bed with one of his squeaky toys. "No, Ricardo. Phone." I said.

Ricardo looked at me with the confidence of a horse winning the Kentucky Derby. Diving on the floor like a duck on a June bug, Ricardo came out triumphant. As he was standing before me with the cell phone clinched in his mouth, Ricardo's tail was wagging with conviction and with assurance he was here to stay.

I know, I know, you're thinking what does a handsome, smart well-trained dog have to do with having partners in life? Hold on, it's coming. For Ricardo to be a successful canine companion, he needed partners in life. He needed trainers in his life to provide training so he would be the best he could be.

Ricardo was born in California. There a group of people made sure of his health while assessing his performance. They graded him on how much energy he displayed, how willing he was to please people, how playful he was, how his attitude was after being corrected, and other valuable attributes required to be a service canine.

When Ricardo was old enough to travel, he was flown to Mississippi to be puppy raised. For the next eighteen months, Ricardo resided in one of Mississippi's prisons where he learned the basic training. There his partner, a prisoner, worked and trained Ricardo to sit, stand, shake, which side to be on, the left or the right, if he wanted Ricardo in the down position, when it's appropriate to use the restroom, and other commands. After his prison stay, it's time to move to Florida.

Orlando is the final training for Ricardo. He learned to retrieve items from the floor, to turn lights off and on, open and close doors and drawers, and how to be a companion.

Ricardo had a lot of partners to make sure

he would be successful. It was not one or two partners but multiple partners. Each one had a specific goal or expertise, which allowed Ricardo to perform to his highest capability.

Like a new puppy we need multiple partners in our life. Not just a spouse, a significant other, or a friend, even though they are very important in our lives, but many people who will help us become better than we ever thought we could be. "It takes a village to raise a child." Not only is that true but it is also essential to us as well.

When we surround ourselves with people who can support us by developing our character, self-esteem, confidence, morals, and other inner traits, then we can mold our minds for greatness. This is known as a mastermind group. There are different names for this type of group but the process is the same. As Brian Tracy was once quoted, "No one lives long enough to learn everything they need to learn starting from scratch. To be successful, we absolutely, positively have to find people who have already paid the price to learn the things that we need to learn to achieve our goals." Each person in the assembly brings something beneficial to the group. Everybody is to share ideas, encouragement, positive criticism that might spark a new concept or a thought that could assist in developing of everybody's success or assist in overcoming adversities.

Your spouse or significant other should be willing to support and encourage you during your dreams and failures. Not only will they entertain your inspirations but also they will sacrifice something in their lives to assure the best possibility of your dream coming true no matter the difficulties.

Other partners in your circle of survival should be special friends. This friend is the one who will tell you the truth about your next great idea. They will encourage you to try and will give you the positives and negatives about your thought. They will provide you with an emotional crutch so you can stay tall while staying positive. Kelly Clarkson stated, "My friends and family are my support system. They tell me what I need to hear, not what I want to hear and they are there for me in the good and bad times. Without them I have no idea where I would be and I know that their love for me is what's keeping my head above the water."

When you have a dilemma that is causing a distraction, this friend will play the devil's advocate to help you understand if the goals to become successful are appropriate. They might imply, "This is not for me but I can see you doing it." They will support you without hesitation and without limits.

If you are starting a new relationship, your friend will be there to tell the truth about the person you are dating because of the saying "Love is blind," by Geoffrey Chaucer. The friend will tell it like it is to put you back in reality. Again, they are not to be negative, hurt you, or be afraid if you succeed you might leave them behind. They want what is best for you and they will help by being bluntly truthful.

Staying healthy during your life is essential. If you are in poor health, it will be harder to achieve your goals or stay positive after a challenge in life. By staying strong and as healthy as possible, you can stay focused on your ambitions. While some people are self-motivated to maintain their health, most need a partner or partners to provide encouragement to exercise, eat nutritional meals, get the right amount of sleep, and stay mentally healthy. These partners might be your physician, a trainer, a nutritionist, a life coach and/or a psychologist or a psychiatrist. If the mind is healthy, it will be easier to help the body stay strong and healthy as well. Buddha was quoted, "To keep the body in good health is a duty... otherwise we shall not be able to keep our mind strong and clear."

This is a weird partner to have but you need someone who will build your ego. "The purpose of human life is to serve, and to show compassion and the will to help others," Albert Schweitzer said. This person will agree with you on everything you say, no matter if it is beneficial to you or not. They will be the ones who will make you feel good when times are bad. They worship your friendship. They are afraid if you get mad at them you will discontinue the relationship so it's easier to just agree with you. Even though they make you feel good, you have the other friends who will slap you into reality.

Another partner most people do not think about is a mentor or a life coach. Find someone who has the same desire as yours or who has been down the same road you're traveling. Have a meeting with them and ask for advice about your topic or challenges. Research them to see if they are really successful in helping people persevere. After learning about them, asked if they will mentor you. You never know unless you ask. Be careful, there are plenty of people who will give you advice that you want to hear but they have never done what they're advising.

With the Internet, seminars, teleseminars, webinars, workshops, and libraries, whatever your desires are, you can research the topic or topics. Along with the information collected and the suggestions from all partners involved, it will be easier to make an educated decision. If your expectations are realistic, your partners will support your ambitions and your dreams or goals. Whether you succeed or fail with your adventure, you will know that the best intentions and effort were delivered. By having multiple partners in life, it will be easier to Persevere Past *your* Paralysis.

Strategies to Implement:

1. Make a list of who will be your partner or partners during any circumstance.
2. Remember, this is a group who will assist you during good times as well as bad times.
3. Find out with your friends if you are on their partner list. If not and you know

you can help, sit down and have a talk with them to ensure you can be a great supporting partner.

4. During your situation, study different people who have been through similar problems. Learn their valuable techniques that they used to overcome adversities.

"Being in control of your life and having realistic expectations about your day-to-day challenges are the keys to stress management, which is perhaps the most important ingredient to living a happy, healthy and rewarding life."
- Marilu Henner

Chapter 5
Power

"When I was younger, I thought that the key to success was just hard work. But the real foundation is faith. Faith--the idea that 'I can do it'--is the opposite of fear ('What if I fail?'). And faith creates motivation which in turn leads to commitment, hard work, preparation...and eventually success."
- Howard Twilley

What fires you up? What deep down in your stomach is so hungry for success that it demands your attention to get started? What or where do you gain the strength to assist you during trials and tribulations? Something from within has to inspire you to stay positive, provide encouragement, and remain hopeful. Motivation by itself is no good without initiative. Something within must ignite the desire to want to destroy difficulties. What power kick starts the initiative in your life to achieve in life's struggle? You must be self-motived; if you do not have the burning desire to do or want the best you deserve, motivation minus initiative equals no results. Tony Robbins inspired others by saying, "Success comes from taking the initiative and following up... persisting... eloquently expressing the depth of your love. What simple action could you take today to produce a new momentum toward success in your life?" People have different power techniques they use to deliver initiative to get results.

This chapter is not to persuade anyone to any certain belief, it is not to try to change your religious denomination, and not to offend anyone. Whether you believe in and pray to God or not; it is not my objective to change your mind one way or another. You might believe in another type of religion, maybe you do yoga or some other type of meditation. Whatever makes you respond to challenges, use it to the fullest to persevere.

There are many different beliefs and ways to fire people up to attain the much needed desire to overcome adversities. You must decide and know what it is that works for you. Personally, I thank God for providing me with the strength and initiative to accept my daily challenges and life long struggles from being a quadriplegic.

When life becomes challenging or even unbearable, most people turn to a higher object greater than themselves, God. They pray for the strength, the understanding, the guidance, the power, the perseverance, and everything you can think of to be able to accept the tragedy they are experiencing during that time.

There are people who believe and pray what I call "straight forward prayers." They reflect on scripture such as "For I know the plans I have for you," declares the Lord, "plans to prosper you and not to harm you, plans to give you hope and a future." Jeremiah 29:11; "For God so loved the world that He gave His one and only Son, that whoever believes in Him shall not perish but have eternal life." John 3:16; and/or "Take delight in the Lord, and He will give you the desires of your heart" Psalm 37:4. They are trying to find healing along with comfort from their suffering. They know that our God has promised us that we will attain more in life than only trials and tribulations.

The Bible is the written word from God and is used to insure us that by staying faithful and strong in life we will be blessed abundantly.

Some people believe and pray in ways I call, "negative but I meant it as a positive prayer." I'm thankful our God is a big strong God. We question Him about our challenges whether the problem is big or small. People question God to figure out what or why a certain trial has happened to them, for example; How can You say You love me and allow my suffering? When is tragedy a desire of my heart? I thought I was your favorite so why do You consent to the travesties in my families' lives? Why me?

A third group of people go to God and His word on a positive platform by using verses like these; "I have told you these things, so that in me you may have peace. In this world you will have trouble. But take heart! I have overcome the world." John 16:33. "Consider it pure joy, my brothers and sisters, whenever you face trials of many kinds, because you know that the testing of your faith produces perseverance. Let perseverance finish its work so that you may be mature and complete, not lacking anything." James 1:2-4. "He will wipe every tear from their eyes. There will be no more death' or mourning or crying or pain, for the old order of things has passed away." Revelation 21:4. Even though a misfortune has taken place, these people stay positive and expect greater outcomes are coming from their hardship. Staying positive will help them get through their troubles while having a better understanding of the situation. They understand that going through an undesirable adventure will prepare them for future surprises.

The final group, and I think the largest, is the ones who participate in a combination of the three. These people know the verses to quote and pray while questioning God on the circumstance and staying faithful with more of a positive attitude than a negative one. They look at the reality of the adversity on whether it is imposed on them or if by design they brought it on themselves. For me, I fall into this group.

By staying positive, my go-to verses are, "You intended to harm me, but God intended it for good to accomplish what is now being done, the saving of many lives. So then, don't be afraid. I will provide for you and your children." Genesis 50:19-21. Also, "We know that in all things God works for the good of those who love him, who have been called according to his purpose." Romans 8:28. Finally, "but those who hope in the LORD will renew their strength. They will soar on wings like eagles; they will run and not grow weary, they will walk and not be faint." Isaiah 40:31. Again it is a good thing God is big enough that when I asked, "What's the purpose for me to be a quadriplegic?"

After thirty years of being in a wheelchair, this question can be partially answered. When first attending college I had no intentions of graduating. Low and behold with a "C" average in high school it is only because of my injury that completing a doctoral degree was attainable, traveling to Africa and other countries was possible. Reaching people with inspiration is now my desire. Such as finding out by a person who was incarcerated in the county jail that she had read my first book, *One More Play*, located in the jail's library.

March 15th, 2014, was National Storytelling Day. Ricardo, my service canine, and I were invited to share a story of how we became companions. My story was about overcoming adversities and difficulties. We will all have challenges in life that will push us to our limits – at least we think. Sometimes we need someone to help us through our tragedies – a spouse, a doctor, a friend, or a family member – that was basically my presentation.

On this day, unknowingly, I would be providing the inspiration this woman, a stranger, needed. With only eight minutes to tell how I got paralyzed, my diagnoses, and my accomplishments it was time for everyone to meet Ricardo. He demonstrated how he assists my needs and like always, Ricardo stole my thunder – ha!

After the day and all the programs were over, there was time to meet and greet the storytellers and authors. A woman whom I believe to be in her late fifties maybe early sixties, came to talk with me. She explained she was dealing with an issue in life. While listening to my story, she told me I had provided her the inspiration and encouragement that she needed to help with her situation. I thanked her for her kind words. She hugged me and left quietly.

A few days later a friend sent me an e-mail. While reading, I felt overwhelmed by the information. The woman who attended the storytelling event had received news from her doctor just four days before we met she had terminal cancer. She did not have long to live.

Reading the e-mail, I could not help but believe it was God's plan for her to be there that day during my presentation.

You never know what's going on in other people's lives and you do not know when you have helped them through the day, unless they approach to tell you, so we need to provide the encouragement one needs because someone else will do the same for you one day when it's your turn.

When a family gets kicked in the teeth from life, what's there to do? A mother and father decide to assist other families to make their struggles full of love and care. They started an organization in memory of their son in hopes they can make life easier for families who have a child in the hospital. Be sure to tell your mother you love her on Mother's Day and remember Isaac's story.

Simply Making Isaac's Laugh Eternal (S.M.I.L.E.), Inc. was founded in honor of Isaac who was diagnosed with Acute Lymphoblastic Leukemia (ALL) which was complicated by a rare genetic. Isaac was always known for his quick wit and endless humor. Even through cancer, he continued to be quite the charmer. Isaac was sixteen years old when he was diagnosed and was so humbled by the gifts and cards he received from total strangers while in the hospital.

He said, "That's cool. When I get better, I'm gonna do this."

Isaac went to be with Jesus less than five months after his fight for his life began. So, Isaac is better now and this is how he is continuing to make other kids smile.

S.M.I.L.E. benefits the families at Monroe Carell Jr. Children's Hospital at Vanderbilt, when their worlds have been turned upside down after their children have been diagnosed with cancer. Childhood cancer is treated much differently than adulthood cancer and often there is no known cause. Children treated with chemotherapy are at a higher risk of developing other cancers within their lifetime. Radiation treatments often leave children infertile. With hospital admissions often and sometimes lasting for months, four months in the event of a transplant, families are often reduced to one income when they once required two. Household expenses can double with soaring gas prices, food costs, and medical bills.

S.M.I.L.E. will provide care packages that will include toiletries, SOFT toilet tissue, laundry detergent and goods, basic necessities, snacks, and some items for entertainment value (magazines, puzzle books, journals, cards, etc.) They will also provide age appropriate and personalized gifts for the children. They include gas cards, gift cards for groceries and restaurants that are in or close to VCH. They even help out with utility bills, etc. in extreme cases. Sometimes the most meaningful thing that they can do for a family is just sit and talk with them, play games with the children, and let them know that they are not alone.

There is an annual "Fishin' for Isaac" Big Fish Bass Tournament every year. The proceeds are used to buy supplies for the children and families who stay at Vanderbilt Children's Hospital. For more information about S.M.I.L.E. go to: http://www.smile4isaac.org

Isaac's parents turned a horrible situation into a powerful tool. They are helping many people in depressing and unfavorable circumstances while educating others about their loved one Isaac. Through S.M.I.L.E. Isaac is providing happiness, encouragement and a bit of hope during a bitter tasting point in these families lives.

Think about the power you can produce to

gain the inner strength needed to persevere through difficult times. Whatever works for you might not do the same for another person. This power will help you with not only the strength to endure adversities but also assist with making problem-solving decisions. This newly found power would build or restore confidence that has been missing from your life. After a collection of small victories, along with the fresh confidence, friends and family might want to know your secret. While explaining the new habit or behavior, you are in the position of helping them. Use your powers wisely, Grasshopper, as you Persevere Past *your* Paralysis.

Strategies to Implement:

1. Discover your inner strength. What provides the power you need daily and especially during your suffering?
2. Whatever gives you the power on a daily basis or sometimes a minute-by-minute survival test, continue going to it and using it.

The partner that you have is supposed to make

you a better person, and when you're happy,
you're a better person.
- Bai Ling

Chapter 6
Perseverance

Great works are performed not by
strength but by perseverance.
- Samuel Johnson

"Ain't No Stopping Us Now, We're On The Move" a song by Luther Vandross could be a great theme to encourage someone to go forward. It does not matter how fast you are going; a snail's pace is perfect as long as you're moving forward. Just push through the hardship glass doors or in some cases plow forward and break them open. There might be a time when you moved one step forward and then two steps back. That is not the worst thing in the world to have happen. By stepping back, it gives you more time to make sure the goals you set are stable, it forces you to focus on your dream, or it may help you evaluate the challenge for a better solution. Get fired up and stay the course. Soon you can play the song "The Future's So Bright, I Gotta Wear Shades" by Timbuk 3.

While persevering, do not be afraid to step back and remember where you were in life. That way you'll notice how far you have advanced. The light at the end of a tunnel will not look or feel as if a train is coming when you weathered the storm and the bright light of overcoming obstacles is filling up your face. Stand tall with confidence and know you have put forward the best effort possible.

Helen Keller once said, "Although the world is full of suffering, it is full also of the overcoming of it." College was to be Terry's ticket to freedom. It was also expected from his parents that both of their children would go to college and graduate. Unfortunately, Terry's SAT scores were very low. He tried numerous colleges that seemed appropriate for him, but it seemed that he was not "appropriate" for them. Finally, a small school in central North Carolina gave Terry that letter of acceptance that he had so anxiously awaited.

Terry's parents, like all anxious parents, waved goodbye to him for it was time to start school, his freedom. Terry turned up the stereo and was "free at last." This new experience of being on his own was extremely overwhelming. The social activities of dorm life and fraternity parties didn't leave much time for scholastics. After a semester and a half, Terry's father became tired of sending him to "fun 101" since Terry didn't keep up his end of the deal by passing classes so they didn't pay for the next semester of classes. Tears came down his face as they pulled out of the college driveway. Terry started to wonder what he would do now.

Terry decided to give college another try, but closer to home. He picked up some classes at West Virginia University (WVU) in pursuit of a degree in psychology. Due to Terry's "proud" performance of academia the first time, his GPA was less than a 2.0, he was only allowed to take a few classes. He guessed he had to prove that he had the "old college try" in perspective.

The next two years at WVU Terry was putting at least a half a foot forward into the academics. He had cracked the 2.0 barrier and managed to have a fairly good social life. He enjoyed school and became involved in his psychology degree by helping other graduate students with their research, grunt work. It really provided him with a firm sense that he wanted to help others via his degree. About halfway into his junior year, Terry's credits were all out of order so he took the summer looking for a job. His father had just acquired some property up in northern Canada; Terry's childhood dreams were about to come true.

Terry's dad wanted to build a cottage, nestled in the trees, and looking out upon the lake, kind of an "On Golden Pond" feature. Terry's friend Sean and his cousin Todd were also jobless, so Terry proposed to his father that they help build the cottage. They loaded Terry's vehicle with hammers, nails, paints and other building materials. When Terry met the foreman, he was told that "black muck" was found where the cottage was to be built. The best way to describe it was like black Jell-O. The land had to be cleared out before they could proceed with building the cottage.

Well, that gave Terry about a week to do nothing but fish, how relaxing. As May was coming to an end, the weather began to warm and presenting a far greater problem than he could ever realize... black flies. These things can eat you alive and practically drive you crazy. The Canadians were used to them, but to Terry it was pure hell. They were told not to wear anything fragrant because it would attract flies. After about two weeks of stinking, they decided it was time to clean up and do laundry.

"For we pay a price for everything we get or take in this world; and although ambitions are well worth having, they are not to be cheaply won" according to Lucy Maud Montgomery. While driving back from their laundry excursion from a remote Indian town, Terry told his friends to be on the lookout for wildlife. Turning a corner, Terry's headlights fell upon some unexpected wildlife; a bull moose was standing in the middle of the road. Terry locked his brakes and told his friends that they were going to hit it. As the car came to a stop, Terry called out to see if they were all right. They said they were, but how was Terry? Terry could not move. His head was bent down to his chest because the roof of the car was on it.

After the fifteen hundred pound moose was off the car, Terry's friends tried pulling the roof off him. He told them that would be futile plus he did not need to be moved. A passing car was flagged down and took Terry's cousin back to town for help. The nearest ambulance was sixty miles away and would end up taking an hour and a half to get to Terry. As he was sitting in the car, a lot of thoughts went through his mind. How badly hurt was he? Did he have any cuts on head? Was he going to live? Terry felt a peace of mind come over him; he was ready to accept his fate in life.

Terry found that he had a spinal cord injury and he became a quadriplegic. He couldn't move from his neck down and required twenty-four hours assistance seven days a week. After two months in intensive care at a Toronto hospital, he went back to his hometown of Pittsburgh, Pennsylvania, for rehabilitation. Terry's family and friends were very supportive, expecting nothing more than the same old Terry. As he began his rehabilitation, Terry began to think about his future. John Quincy Adams said, "Patience and perseverance have a magical effect before which difficulties disappear and obstacles vanish. A little knowledge that acts is worth infinitely more than much knowledge that is idle."

Terry had completed over half of his college credits so he decided to contact his college advisor and tell him what happened. They were able to work out an independent study project. Terry didn't want to waste any more time, he want to continue to pursue his college degree. He was even more determined to work in a field of helping others.

The campus at WVU was too hilly to navigate so he was able to work out a program with WVU and the University of Pittsburgh to take classes at Pitt. The credits would be transferred to WVU. That summer he began classes at Pitt. He spent the next couple of years completing his education and graduated in 1980. Terry was very proud and glad that he had completed his undergraduate degree in psychology. He was now ready to hit the job market and he thought that surely somebody would hire a college graduate.

For two years Terry worked at a county-run nursing facility, but it just wasn't what he wanted. He completed an application to attend Pitt's School of Counselor Education and the School of Social Work so he could receive his master's degree. He was accepted to the social work program with an emphasis on counseling. Keep in mind that during his bachelors program Terry was basically a "C" student. He was now forced to a higher level of learning, which means that he needed to become an "A – B" student. After eighteen months of intense education,

Terry had done it. He earned a Masters in Social Work.

Terry was able to work in such settings as rehabilitation hospitals, community mental health, advocacy programs, and the State Department of Health of Tennessee. Terry was able to look back at a traumatic event that has impacted his life greatly in a very positive way. Terry knew that he could accomplish what he set out to do regardless of his "disability," which at many times is very much an "ability." Tragedy can strike when you least expect it and in the most unexpected fashion like a fifteen hundred pound moose on your head. It is how one uses this experience and turns it into a positive that makes them a "winner." Terry overcame adversity, which he thought would be impossible; Terry became a "winner" for persevering when life looked bleak.

"Adversity is like a strong wind. I don't mean just that it holds us back from places we might otherwise go. It also tears away from us all but the things that cannot be torn, so that afterward we see ourselves as we really are, and not merely as we might like to be," wisely stated by Arthur Golden. Terry finally saw greatness in himself due to a tragic event. Not that we would wish harm on our fellow man or woman but sometimes when difficulties happen we find out how we are made.

Even though Terry could not move from his neck down and was totally dependent on others to assist him with his entire daily needs, he accomplished more than most people who have all functions and control of their body and mind. Sadly, Terry died in 2009 leaving life-long memories of how to live and overcome challenges, even though a fifteen hundred pound moose did its best, it could not stop him.

"What lies behind us and what lies before us are tiny matters compared to what lies within us," Ralph Waldo Emerson stated. Terry used his tragedy to power the needed determination and stayed fired up to persevere through his troubled circumstance. How many would want to live knowing their daily needs are in other people's hands? Who would want to survive knowing when it is time to evacuate the bowels and bladder someone else is in control of the cleanup? Terry could only blink his eyes and open his mouth but thankfully his mind was not damaged so he could operate his power chair and educated others with his wise knowledge while encouraging everyone he came in contact with.

Zig Ziglar, widely world-known motivational speaker, once said, "You were designed for accomplishment, engineered for success, and endowed with the seeds of greatness." If and when misfortunes happen, when it is said and done, how did you handle your circumstance? Did it destroy you and your life or did you do the best you could despite the adversity? Sometimes the hardest thing to do is get out of bed the next day when being overwhelmed with hardship.

There are plenty of people who are betting that you will fold. They are so insecure with themselves and their lives they want everyone to suffer along with them. Don't allow their lack of self-worth to brainwash you to think the same about yourself. "It's a lie to think you're not good enough. It's a lie to think you're not worth anything," author of the book *Life Without Limbs* Nick Vujicic courageously related. Do not give them the pleasure of knowing how bad you are doing. Do not be afraid to ask for help when striving for better in your life. You must persevere through life.

The next story is one that most people will never experience unless you pack up your belongings and move to another country. Being a foreigner is hard enough even if one researches the country but moving there can be an eye opening, undeserving, bad situation.

Kim Kim was born and raised in the Buddhist temple in Korea. At the age of seventeen years old, he moved to America as an exchange student. It was not easy for him as he endured some fellow students and co-workers making fun and bullying him due to his lack of verbal speaking skills along with the lack of knowledge of American customs.

Even though Kim Kim is from Korea, a few of American classmates who were ignorant in their own world history classes would imply with prejudices to "go back to China," or call him "Chinese." The same few people who would laugh at him for no particular reason even though they displayed the lack of knowledge where he was from.

Not only being unable to speak the language but also the culture shock of America was surprising. Kim Kim was used to staying in one classroom for about ninety percent of the day including eating lunch there. The only ever-changing view for the day was when different teachers would enter the classroom to educate the students. The first day at his new high school was a brain buster as there were more cars in the parking lot than teachers. In Korea, students were not permitted to drive to school whereas in America it is acceptable.

Despite not knowing or having limited English understanding, he persevered and graduated high school. Not letting his language challenge be a barrier, he later earned a bachelor degree from Middle Tennessee State University. He owned several businesses until accepting a position as a director in a hospital.

After becoming a Rotary club member, he became the fourth Korean-American District Governor in North America and the first in Tennessee. As a ShelterBox Response member, Kim Kim has been recognized for his humanitarian efforts by helping those in natural disasters. Also, he has traveled to five continents to execute Rotary projects including National Immunization Day in Africa, the dental/vision/medical mission in Guatemala, and the electricity project in Honduras. He received the President's Volunteer Service Award from President Barack Obama, Rotary's highest honor, the Service Above Self Award, the Tennessee Hospital Association Meritorious

Service Award, and many more. He returned to Korea to marry his wife Sue in an arranged marriage. Kim Kim and Sue have three children.

As a misfit, according to the stupidity of a few uneducated people, Kim Kim has overcome complications by persevering and not allowing some discriminated intolerant selected few people to bully him around. It would be interesting if Kim Kim and his backward thinking ex-classmates could meet and see who has achieved the most in life.

When persevering, remember, it's not a race. You don't have to act at one hundred miles an hour. It's perfectly acceptable to move at a snails pace. Keep moving forward and onward. Robert Downing Jr. said, "I think that the power is the principle. The principle of moving forward, as though you have the confidence to move forward, eventually gives you confidence when you look back and see what you've done."

In the summer of 1986, about fifteen people with disabilities from Tennessee Rehabilitation Center decided to participate in the area Paralympics competition. I signed up for two swimming events that were held indoors. Watching other people swim started my adrenalin pumping. Before I knew it, my first swimming event had approached. While watching my competitors practice, the need to feel sorry for them became evident because they looked weak and uncoordinated from their limitations. Even though thinking it would not be fair to embarrass them, I had to do what I had to do.

The only swimming we could do was the backstroke. We potentially could drown if we tried to swim face down because we cannot turn our heads to get our mouths out of the water to take a breath. It was time to climb out of my wheelchair and sit on the floor. Then, traveling to the final destination – the water.

We were in the water with our arms on the side of the pool and all of a sudden the horn sounded to start the race. Pushing off the wall with all my might I started my backstroke while still thinking this was not going to be pretty. And I was right! This was not pretty at all!

The sporting competition, not felt in me for nearly three years, kicked in. The sound of the crowd made my adrenalin flow throughout my partially paralyzed muscle. In the water, feeling light weight and agile, I was swimming like no one else's business. During the race, hitting the game winning homerun emotions immerged, the excitement of pitching a no hitter came to mind, and the awards earned during my sporting career were indications that hard work, determination, and the competitive drive was still in me. I was playing the song *Eye of the Tiger* by Survivor from Rocky in my mind. This was great! This is a sport to participate in and learn to love.

When looking to my left and then to my right there was no vision of anybody in the other lanes. I was beating them so bad they were nowhere in sight – what a great feeling. About halfway through the race, my arms were burning and hurting. I had hit the wall, not the pool wall, but my energy was depleted and wasn't going anywhere. The crowd was cheering, but the harder my attempt to swim the less movement in the pool became apparent. After swimming stationary in the water, the thought of grabbing one of the lane dividing ropes entered my mind; once my breath was caught it would be time to finish the race.

When reaching for the rope about four able-bodied people dove in the water for the rescue. They transported me to the side of the pool to make sure I was fine and helped me out of the pool into my wheelchair. Then, the realistic reason why no competitor was seen to the left or the right of me was evident because they had all finished the race. Not only was I the only one in the pool at the time, but also to top it off I was the only person dragged out of the pool like a huge catfish on the bottom of a lake. It was embarrassing. Everyone saw me needing assistance and not finishing the race. I pushed my wheelchair out of the pool area like a dog with his tail between his legs into the dressing locker room. As said earlier, this was not going to be pretty. Was I right or was I right?

The recreation director from Tennessee Rehabilitation Center who had organized the trip, friends, and other athletes came to comfort me. Though in tears, I didn't want to hear what they had to say. But there was one recurring phrase; they were saying that I didn't have to swim in the next event. Assuring them that there will be no more swimming and letting them know they could not use reverse psychology to talk me into swimming again. For me to quit something is rare, but getting publicly embarrassed like that again made up my mind that swimming is not for me.

After about fifteen minutes of feeling sorry for myself, an announcement was made that the next swimming race was about to begin. The announcement called for the swimmers in the event by name. When hearing my name I continued saying, "I am not going out there." After hearing my name for the second time, there still was no movement to the pool.

The final call was made, "James Perdue come to the pool or you will be disqualified." Since I had never forfeited, nor been disqualified, nor quit a game before, the competitive spirit in me would not allow me to go out like this. Eleanor Roosevelt once said, "You gain strength, courage and confidence by every experience in which you really stop to look fear in the face; You must do the thing you think you cannot do."

I pushed back to the pool and repeated the effort like before entering the water and getting ready for the race – or at least – trying to finish. The second race could have been a replay of the first. The exact same thing happened.

About halfway down the lane my arms were giving out, the hurting and burning reappeared, and it seemed as if I was frozen in the water. This time from an early lesson learned DO NOT grab the rope. Dale Turner mused, "Some of the best lessons are learned from past mistakes. The error of the past is the wisdom of the future."

So swimming was the plan or at least moving my arms even though the lack of propelling in the water was obvious. "The most authentic thing about us is our capacity to create, to overcome, to endure, to transform, to love, and to be greater than our suffering," according to Ben Okri. Then, hit by an inspiration, not in my head at first but in my foot. My toes touched the bottom of the pool so I decided to use my strength in my legs and push off the pool floor. When moving my arms in a swimming motion simultaneously my legs kicked off the bottom of the pool. People thought I had reenergized and they were cheering even louder. On a mission like no other to finish the race, while moving only three or four feet at a time, there was no stopping me now. So you are thinking he cheated and it can be looked at that way, but I view it as exploring all my options and using my creativity to complete the race.

At the end of your time on Earth, what will count the most is how you live and how you helped your fellow people. Abraham Lincoln once said, "In the end it's not the years in your life that count. It's the life in your years." People will remember the times in your life when you stayed the course, persevering and not quitting. Thomas A. Edison once said, "Our greatest weakness lies in giving up. The most certain way to succeed is always to try just one more time." They will talk about the strength you endure during trials and tribulations in your life while secretly you provided them the power to overcome difficulties. Unknowingly, they admired you for your quest to be persistent to conquer and destroy the misfortunes in life while learning from your fortitude to be successful in life because you Persevere Past *your* Paralysis.

Strategies to Implement:

1. Remember a time when you thought you could go no farther due to a tragedy. How did you feel when you decided to push on and eventually you were able to survive that tough time?

2. At the time of adversity, the road looks and seems long. Persevering though the challenges can be difficult. Choose a motivation you can depend on that

will assist you in moving forward.

The price of success is hard work, dedication to the job at hand, and the determination that whether we win or lose, we have applied the best of ourselves to the task at hand.
-Vince Lombardi

Chapter 7
Prevail Your Life

"Nothing in the world can take the place of persistence. Talent will not; nothing is more common than unsuccessful men with talent. Genius will not; unrewarded genius is almost a proverb. Education will not; the world is full of educated derelicts. Persistence and determination alone are omnipotent. The slogan, 'press on' has solved, and always will solve, the problems of the human race."
- Calvin Coolidge

Congratulations for almost completing this book because most people who start books even if they are on audio, CD and/or DVD programs do not finish. Can I promise there will be no challenges in your life after the conclusion? Of course not, but I can say with confidence by implementing these strategies you will be better prepared to handle the situation and eventually overcome the adversity.

Will the tragedies totally vanish? In some cases "yes" and in other cases "no." After sustaining my injury and being paralyzed, I have accomplished more than I ever thought possible after losing the ability to walk, but daily transferring into my wheelchair reminds me of that destructive day. In this case it can be viewed as a doubled-edged sword. On one side of the sword it can be a reminder of the life loss, as I knew it, the playing baseball dream, the limited independence, the negative aspects from the event.

The other side of the sword can be viewed as the positive side. Finding the silver lining in the clouds. Try taking a bad situation and transforming it for the good. What about living a life to the best of my ability and trying to achieve dreams that few people ever dream? Rose Kennedy beautifully said, "Birds sing after a storm; why shouldn't people feel as free to delight in whatever sunlight remains to them?" That paralyzing day was a devastating life-changing episode in my life. There are plenty of people in similar situations that gave up on life whereas after the dust settled, in my view, it is a blessing.

A blessing? Sure, walking would be a preferable outcome. Losing the ability to take steps has slowed me down physically, but continuing to move forward in life is nothing less than miraculous. The drive to achieve is a dominant trait that I wish everybody would master. Other than being created equal with a sperm cell and an egg cell from our fathers and mothers, we grow and develop differently. Thomas Jefferson tells us, "We hold these truths to be self-evident: that all men are created equal; that they are endowed by their Creator with certain unalienable rights; that among these are life, liberty, and the pursuit of happiness."

I'll buy into the latter part, "that they are endowed by their Creator with certain unalienable rights; that among these are life, liberty, and the pursuit of happiness," but not the opening statement, "We hold these truths to be self-evident: that all men are created equal." If we are created equal, why are some people born with disabilities, different learning styles, economical differences, or dissimilar IQ levels?

Harper Lee, To Kill a Mockingbird, responded with, "We know all men are not created equal in the sense some people would have us believe – some people are smarter than others, some people have more opportunity because they're born with it, some men make more money than others, some ladies make better cakes than others – some people are born gifted beyond the normal scope of men. But there is one way in this country in which all men are created equal – there is one human institution that makes a pauper the equal of a Rockefeller, the stupid man the equal of an Einstein, and the ignorant man the equal of any college president. That institution, gentlemen, is a court." Most of the poor population will remain poor while very few of the rich will lose everything. Can both scenarios happen? You bet your magic genie lamp it can. One thing that is equal is that everybody will suffer and have undesirable tragedies in life. There are different ways of coping with challenges.

If you are one of those people who think they have never had tragedy in their life that is great, but sad at the same time. Looking at life realistically, if people live long enough, they will face circumstances unfavorable. If they feel they have never experienced a disaster, when a catastrophe finally happens, will they know how to deal with it? Whether it is the loss of a loved one, health issues, or whatever the situation, not only will they not be prepared on how to accept and adjust to the change in life, but also not know how to react to the setback during that time.

When we are young we learn to adapt to change and better prepare ourselves for future difficulties. According to Les Brown, "When life knocks you down, try to land on your back. Because if you can look up, you can get up. Let your reason get you back up." When we win, even the small fight, we gain encouragement and strength to tackle the big problems.

Sometimes we must fail to be successful. Defeat lets us know if we really want what we desire. People talk a good game when it comes to success but to actually walk the talk is totally different. Words are just that "words." If I tell you how to become successful but I've never followed my own advice, then how many people will take the advice and run with it? People want to see results or the words in action. Just because someone can talk baseball does not mean he has ever won a World Series.

We learn from failure. We're cruising right along crossing off the goals that have been completed. Then, out of nowhere, a specific goal is unattainable. Failure has slipped into our world. What to do? We learn from the failure. We know the course of direction has to change. Take the information already known and develop a new goal, pause and come back to that goal, or drop and punt. Remember, some of your goals or plans do not have a time table so let them sit and come back to them with more information and a better chance for success.

Struggles will come. The saying is by Tom Hanks, "If it wasn't hard, everyone would do it. It's the hard that makes it great." Success is not easy and being successful does not come without a price. Philosopher Kahlil Gibran wrote, "Out of suffering have emerged the strongest souls; the most massive characters are seared with scars." Most people we cannot see their scars because those scars are emotional or mental, but that does not mean they have not gone through difficulties.

Even though pain is not fun or wanted, the great thing is that pain is temporary. It may seem like a lifetime during the process but in reality it may last only for days, a week, a month or even a year. In time, it will be replaced with the confidence, the courage, the strength, the knowledge and the drive to persevere. When the next challenge approaches, it will be easier to conquer. People are watching and learning from how you persist through life. They want to know how and/or where you get the power to go to the next level in life after struggling. They might even say or at least think, "I could not do what you do."

As I was entering one of the buildings at Volunteer State Community College, a fellow student approached me by saying, "I could not do it."

I responded, "Could not do what?"

He replied, "I could not do all the work you just did in the rain and attend class."

I told him, "I have two choices in life. One, I could stay at home and not experience what the world has to offer. Second, I could try to do what I can and be a productive citizen in society. I pick the second option."

People search most of their lives not learning their purpose, while on the other hand, others find their sense of purpose early and discover other possibilities in their lives. Fear can keep you from achieving your dreams. Even though you believe in your future and have a positive attitude, fear can hold you back and keep you from being who you are meant to be.

I've seen people become paralyzed because of the fear they developed. Many people have the fear of failing, the fear of making mistakes, and even, which it is hard to believe, the fear of success. "Fear is met and destroyed with courage," James F. Bell once said. Fear will come and you can either be paralyzed by not taking chances or you can use it to help achieve your goals.

Some fears are useful. For example, fear can be used to motivate athletes to step up their game. The fear of getting hurt prevents most people from doing something stupid. Fear provides the opportunity to fight or flight depending on the circumstances. Fear can be so strong that it actually provides courage to be brave enough to battle a bad situation and triumph over it.

Motivation can be created from fear. For example, when you were younger you might have been motivated to get a good grade on a test because you were fearful your parent would take away some freedom, maybe take away your favorite game, or ground you to stay at home instead of going with your friends. Motivation driven by fear can produce the necessary confidence to take a chance in life to pursue a dream. You see your future spouse from across the room. Fearful of rejection, do you take the chance and ask her on a date?

When fear comes, have the courage to pursue your dreams and believe in your abilities to conquer the challenges that come your way. Unexpected opportunities come to those who move forward. Your family and friends may reach out to you by encouraging you, helping you brainstorm through the challenges, or by providing much needed strength when you thought you were weak. Be thankful they are in your life and they are supportive of you.

Sometimes as the world around you seems to be falling apart, you may feel like quitting. There is no reason to quit even when times are tough. Napoleon Hill once said, "Before success comes in any man's life, he's sure to meet with much temporary defeat and, perhaps some failures. When defeat overtakes a man, the easiest and the most logical thing to do is to quit. That's exactly what the majority of men do." Do not quit! That is the easiest thing to do. Sometimes the challenges we think are holding us back are actually making us stronger. Setbacks should be viewed as different ways to accomplish our dreams and pushing through difficulties. We should not quit if things go wrong but look for a new way of achieving our goals. Sometime when we fail, we are directed to a new goal that can benefit us better than our original goal.

Let your imagination for your dreams soar high. Highly motivated Brian Tracy wisely said, "All successful people, men and women, are big dreamers. They imagine what their future could be, ideal in every respect, and then they work every day toward their distant vision, that goal or purpose." Robin S. Sharma also stated, "Dreamers are mocked as impractical. The truth is they are the most practical, as their innovations lead to progress and a better way of life for all of us." Expect challenges and use them to build your character. Learn from the difficulties and do what is necessary to rise above them. Be open minded enough to accept that difficulties may arise and change your dream. Do not be discouraged if you cannot find a solution to your setback because sooner or later the setback could provide numerous answers to the problem. You have to believe anything is possible and that miracles can happen.

Many people are struggling each day and they need to keep in mind that there is a purpose for their lives. You might be going through troubling times. You might get knocked down and may feel you do not have the strength to get back up. I know the feeling. After feeling like life was not worth living any longer, I attempted suicide not once but three different times in three days. Apparently, God has a plan for me and I'm constantly realizing His purpose. Encouraging and helping others is my purpose in life. With me overcoming adversities, teaching others to persevere past their paralysis is my mission.

In the summer of 1986, I was MAD. Mad at the world. Mad at myself. Mad at the paralysis that held my body hostage. So to tackle the anger within, I set a goal of pushing myself a mile in my wheelchair. I hadn't pushed a mile before, but I was in the mood to do something that would help me get stronger and burn this negative attitude away. Before my injury, I marked off half-mile distances from my home that would equal a mile so I could stay in shape for baseball. This way when I pushed a half mile and wheeled the same distance back it would equal a mile. Bear, my brother, pushed me down our gravel driveway and onto the road to start my one-mile journey. I wasn't pushing to set any time record or going for a leisurely stroll. This was a test to see if it was good therapy for me physically and mentally.

The first half-mile was no problem since it was mostly downhill. But then the dilemma became the angled slope of the roads. Roads are built for water runoff, but the road engineers never figured on a large man, in a rolling vehicle – such as a wheelchair. It was a fight to keep my "rolling chariot" out of the ditch! I got to the end of the half-mile, and it was time to go back. I didn't lose much muscle strength on the first half so I thought going back would be okay. It would be hard, but I didn't think it would be too bad. Then I turned around and saw how much uphill work there would be. I couldn't just sit there because it was getting dark, so I headed toward my biggest challenge of the day: the half-mile return of the "Lone Wheeled Stranger!"

As I continued going back home, I could only go about twenty feet before my arms would get tired and sore. I would stop pushing and take a break for a few minutes. This happened numerous times before I finished the mile. About a third of the way back, I noticed a car was following me. Honestly, it was getting dark, and he was making sure I got home safely by flashing his headlights to warn other cars, but I didn't take it that way. Being mad at the world, now I was getting mad at this jerk for following me.

About half way home, a police car came up; knowing the officer, I yelled, "There is a person in the car who wants to rob me or something. He keeps following me." The officer assured me I wasn't being robbed, there were several calls about someone in a wheelchair on the road, and it was getting dark. I explained that I was getting some exercise.

So, the friendly officer, who was there to protect and serve me, followed until I got home. He even had his blue lights flashing! This was an apparent "get away" of a different kind. No doubt, the neighbors had plenty to talk about that night! (This was 1986, a decade before that infamous white bronco chase in California.) I was going about half a mile an hour, and the blue lights were behind me making every stop I was making and moving forward when I was moving forward. During one stop, the officer got out and we discussed finding a place to push so it would be safe for me. Really? I'm no Albert

Einstein, but after this excursion... even I was not anxious to do this again. After about an hour, I got home, and the officer was on his way to protect and serve other people in the city. After that adventure, I started pushing on Volunteer State Community College's campus for the exercise and for the safety.

When we overcome adversities we become stronger from our opportunities and we learn from our experiences. Gandhi said, "Live as if you were to die tomorrow, learn as if you were to live forever." It was no longer an ambition to push a mile on the roads anymore.

I found out what matters in life are the other people's lives we touch and how we finished our journey is what counts. Our lives are like a roller coaster ride. There are ups and downs as we survive the race. When looking back at your life you will remember important events such as birthdays, marrying, having children, just to mention a few. You will remember some sad occasions like death, divorce, other main struggles from life but the great thing about this part of your journey is remembering how you overcame the obstacles. You'll remember how strong you truly were. For example, you can see yourself as Superman facing a train going out of control and you stopped the train before it derailed. You'll be able to view yourself as an Oprah or Dr. Phil because you demonstrated to others watching that it is possible to triumph through trials and tribulations.

I have the drive to persevere, not giving up, through challenges. If something is worth starting, then it should be worth finishing. We all get our power from within ourselves but what provides power for some may not help others. We have spiritual power from within. We have the desire to become successful for our families as well as the need to be a winner. We witnessed our role models overcome difficulties so we know to live we need to keep on keeping on even when we don't think we can.

You can lead a horse to water but you can't make it drink. Only you can take the steps necessary to make your life better. Only you know what's best for your life. Only you can surround yourself with people who can sculpture your character to be positive and have a strong integrity. Only you can take courses whether online or in a classroom to better yourself. Only you can read self-improvements books, get DVD programs, signup for webinars, or attain audio agendas that can assist in developing your life. Only you can... you get the point.

Today is your day to be successful and to begin the rest of your life. Wake-up your desires or ambitions that you required to push through problems. Why not you? You deserve the best and it is attainable. Every day people become sober from drugs and/or alcohol then go on to have a productive life. People leave horrendous situations because they are fed up with suffering. Why not you?

Many have lost love ones through death whether they were expecting it or death happened unexpectedly. At the time grief seems unbearable but somehow they gained strength and overcame it to live their life. So, why not you?

A lot of people have lost employments and lost everything they worked so hard for. Many have filed for bankruptcy. They didn't throw their arms up in the air because of failure and give up but they worked harder to attain success again. Again I ask, "Why not you?"

You are special and greatness is instilled in you. It's not too late to change your life and change your heritage. God created us to be happy, have an abundant life, and not to suffer. Take advantage of the information learned along with benefitting from your partners in life.

If you are on the inner circle of a partners group, you were chosen or you volunteered to provide assistance to make things easier to overcome adversities. When a challenge occurs to your family or friend, you have indirectly been placed in the situation whether you like it or not. Now you are part of the circumstance. What do you do? This next story is the perspective from the caregivers of a person with a disability.

When Kate learned her son was going to be paralyzed the rest of his life, she knew this was going to be a long journey for all of the family. Even though her son was alive, this experience was going to test all of them and their faith. The commitment on the long haul was going to be tough, staying positive on those days of depression would be mentally exhausting, and the unknowing of what's to come would be an eye-opener. She dedicated twenty-four hours a day to care for him by providing bed baths, catheterization every four hours, getting up every two hours to turn her son in the bed so no sores would develop, not only cook to prepare the food but also feed him, and many other daily needs that are required to live while raising two other sons. Not knowing what the future had in store, Kate hoped for the best but she also planned for the worst; she made funeral arrangements in case her son passed away from the injury.

Tim, the older brother, became part of the team as an indirect caregiver as well. He not only provided the muscle by lifting to help dress and transferring into a wheelchair but also supplied valuable advice on what to do for a lifestyle. Before tension got tighter than a hungry python, Tim became the peacemaker and helped with solving the problems. He had the strength, confidence, and faith of more than most people when it came to teaching his brother to drive an automobile again.

Who knows? Tim's paralyzed brother could have been practice for him because eventually he became one of Terry's caregivers. Tim worked with him for nearly ten years. Over time, Tim and Terry became confidantes while helping each other in different areas of life. Terry eventually became part of Tim's family.

If there is ever a need for an autism whisperer, Tim is the man. He has done great work with some autistic children who others have given up on. Tim has used his life training to be more with the children than people who have degrees and certification in this area. Talk about someone wearing multiple hats in life; there is not a big enough hat rack for Tim to place his hats.

Andy, the young brother, came to the table with a different game plan. He also helped with the muscles but his specialty was in the mechanical field. When the wheelchair broke down or needed adjustments Andy placed his surgical hands on it and performed an overall operation to get the chair back in action. He maintained the vehicles so his brother could continue an education while going out in life to live in it not just survive.

It's sad to say, but God prepared Kate, Tim and Andy as well as James before this tragedy happened. Yes, that's right, this is my family. The ones who read *One More Play* figured that out. We were caregivers for my grandfather who had a stroke, heart attack, and one leg amputated. We assisted my grandmother who was a nurse by feeding, cleaning, transferring and pushing my grandfather in his wheelchair. Overall, we were well prepared to deal with the situation except in one area. I was not ready mentally, emotionally, physically or spiritually to do my part – being the one to receive the care.

In the long run of the race, honestly I could not have been successful in life if it were not for God in my life, my supporting family, and the perseverance instilled in me to overcome adversities. The original plan for my life did not play out as desired but when looking back it's not been a bad life. If one thing could be changed, it would be that my family did not have to suffer along with me.

My partner system sacrificed much of their lives for me to be successful. I'm sure you are proud of your family, but I could not have asked for a better family. When God was designing this family, He worked overtime to make sure it was done right.

When it is all said and done; how do you know if you have been successful in life? After surviving tragedies and living beyond challenges from life, what is your measuring stick so you can know if you have accomplished all you can be? Is it your financial status? What about the awards or recognition received? How about the people you touched in life? Were you the main provider for your family? Traveling the world? Discovering a life-changing formula that helps people maintain health? Inventing an apparatus that made life easier for mankind?

Only you can answer the question. We all have our own measuring device in life. To assist you in your calculation, remember money can't buy happiness, fame is only as good as your last starring event, love is no good when you're by yourself, and some friends might be in your corner for a price.

Did you stand tall when a confrontation occurred because your belief was different than others? When a decision was made, did you keep your integrity? Did you get that warm fuzzy feeling in your heart when helping someone?

Part of the key to successful living especially after adversities is that you become the best person you can be, the best parent you can be, the best partner you can be. You fought the best fight in every circumstance, you served your fellow humans whenever possible, and you lived your life the best possible. We all can't be rich in money, rich in acquiring materials, attain celebrity status, win a Super Bowl or World Series, but one item we all can attain is being the best person we can be in every field of our lives. We can be unselfish when it comes to others, we can keep our promises. We can be role models to demonstrate that triumph over trials and tribulations are possible. We can encourage others while becoming a blessing in their lives.

This may be hard to believe but this life has been a complete blessing. From the people I have met to the places traveled as well as the people who inspired me and the ones who received inspiration from me. The journey is partly over and hopefully there are more years to come to encourage and motivate people who are facing challenges in life to Persevere Past *your* Paralysis.

Strategies to Implement:

1. Maintain your motivational searches and continue applying them daily.
2. Discover your long-term purpose in life. Set short-term goals to accomplish and rethink the ones that are important to you. Remember, short-term goals can have a timetable or date when you want them achieved and they are adjustable.

3. Be responsible for your life. Take control of the controllable things.

4. Have strong partners to mastermind with. An army of positive supportive people to help make educational decisions and be encouragement during challenges.

5. Discover your power. What gets you the strength to deal with trials and tribulations?

6. Keep moving forward. Persevere even if is it striving as slow a snail. Just keep moving straight ahead with your head up high.

"Passion is a feeling that tells you: this is the right thing to do. Nothing can stand in my way. It doesn't matter what anyone else says. This feeling is so good that it cannot be ignored. I'm going to follow my bliss and act upon this glorious sensation of joy."
- Wayne Dyer

Dr. James M. Perdue

About the Author

James said, "After learning my family was advised to place me in a nursing home because I would never get any better, I was determined to persevere through life even though I'd become a quadriplegic." My brother Tim gave some wise and encouraging advice by stating, "Use the determination you had for baseball and direct it toward being successful in life."

At age sixteen, James grew-up fast when his father died. He played baseball in high school and received a college scholarship. Concerned about his mother and brothers, he hoped his athletic talent would lead to a financially successful professional baseball career.

Then, one day, while playing a pick-up football game, James was seriously injured and diagnosed a quadriplegic. He asked the doctor, "How bad is it?"

The doctor responded, "Bad enough. You'll never walk again and possibly not move from the neck down."

Thankfully, God placed James within a family that didn't accept such advice. After years of hard work, fortitude, and perseverance, he was able to return to college. After completing his bachelor's degree, it took him three years to land a teaching contract. Prospective employers saw the wheelchair not the applicant. As an educator, James received teaching and coaching awards. Confident, he decided to return to college. After completing his doctoral degree in May 2011, James became a motivational speaker encouraging other people to triumph over tragedies. He knows all of this would not have been possible without God in his life, his family's support, and his personal values – the desire to succeed in life and overcome adversities.

Dr. Perdue believes it is his calling to help other people overcome their challenges knowing, from his life experience, life is worth living. Persevere Past *your* Paralysis provides the principles that James used to overcome adversities and he hopes this book can help others travel through difficulties with confidences and assurances that a better life is in their future.

Author's Books

One More Play

Dr. Perdue's memoir *One More Play* is about how he overcame adversities after becoming a quadriplegic from a football game. He was told he would never walk again and maybe not move from his neck down. His family was advised to place James in a nursing home because he would be too much of a burden to provide care. James went on to become an award-winning educator, state championship coach, a doctorate degree and successful motivational speaker.

Dr. Perdue's four children books are used to educate children about life challenges and health issues. His canine companion Ricardo demonstrates the way in which we should treat people no matter their circumstance.

Never Fear Ricardo is Here

A wheelchair-bound boy named James wants to play baseball but has trouble since he can't run to play in the field. His mother finds an organization that trains dogs to help people with disabilities to be active in society. Ricardo, a canine assistant, aids James not only in baseball but also in life as well.

Can My Son Pet Your Dog?

James and his service canine Ricardo are shopping when an unexpected turn of event takes place. A surprised mother hears her autistic son's first word when he communicates to Ricardo.

Ricardo and Isaac Go Hunting

James and Ricardo find out that Isaac is receiving treatments because he was diagnosed with cancer. After Isaac's treatments, Ricardo is invited to go hunting. Isaac enjoys fishing and hunting while appreciating Mother Nature's works of art.

Have A Merry Ricardo Christmas

Enjoy Christmas as Ricardo helps Santa unpack his bag of goodies. Rudolph and Ricardo meet for the first time. When all is said and done, Ricardo gets his Christmas treats too.

To purchase any of Dr. Perdue's books visit Amazon at www.amazon.com or visit his website at www.JamesPerdueSpeaks.com

For more information about Dr. Perdue as a speaker for your next event:
E-mail: JamesPerdueSpeaks@comcast.net
or visit his website:
www.JamesPerdueSpeaks.com

Stories in this Book

Joanne's story is from an interview.

Ron's story was provided by a friend.

Bobby's story was from interviewing.

Tim's story was from interviewing and personally knowing him.

More information about S.M.I.L.E. visit their website at http://smile4isaac.org

Terry's story was from his manuscript.

Learn more about Kim Kim by going to Amazon and purchase his two books:
> I Am Rotarian
> My Life in Letters: The Extraordinary
>> Journey of an Ordinary Man from
>> Korea

Reader Notes

www.ingramcontent.com/pod-product-compliance
Lightning Source LLC
LaVergne TN
LVHW021502080426
835509LV00018B/2372